T H E
WORLD
WAR
II
QUIZ BOOK

T H E
WORLD
WAR
II
QUIZ BOOK

John Malone

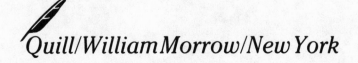

Quill/William Morrow/New York

Copyright © 1991 by John Malone

Library of Congress Cataloging-in-Publication Data

Malone, John Williams.
    The World War II quiz book / John Malone.
        p.   cm.
    ISBN 0-688-10872-5
    1. World War, 1939–1945—Miscellanea. 2. Questions and answers.
  I. Title.
  D743.6.M35   1991
  940.53′076—dc20

                                         91-22556
                                           CIP

Printed in the United States of America

First Quill Edition

BOOK DESIGN BY LISA STOKES

In memory
of my father,
Miles S. Malone, and my uncle,
Dumas Malone

Contents

Part One
1933–1939 Prologue to War

Q. When Adolf Hitler was first appointed chancellor of Germany by its president, the aging World War I hero Field Marshal Paul von Hindenburg, on January 30, 1933, did Hitler's Nazi party hold a majority in the Reichstag (Parliament)?

A. *No. It held only 230 out of 608 seats, but that was the largest bloc.*

Q. What was the contemptuous name by which Hindenburg referred to Hitler?

A. *He called him the Bavarian Corporal. He was pressured into naming Hitler chancellor by industrialists who had made a deal with Hitler. They were fearful of the growing power of the Communists, and agreed to promote Hitler's cause if he would promise to leave German industry to its own devices.*

Q. What was the purpose of the Enabling Act passed by the Reichstag in March of 1933?

A. *It gave Hitler the right to act by decree for four years. He managed to get this through despite the fact that in an elec-*

tion called in March the Nazis still could not win a majority. Right after the election he had most of the Communist deputies arrested, and fear quickly paved the way for the ceding of power to Hitler.

Q. Which was the first to withdraw from the League of Nations, Germany or Japan?

A. *Japan withdrew in March of 1933 because of the League's protests concerning the Japanese establishment of a puppet government in Manchuria. Germany withdrew in October of 1933 when Hitler made a fuss about the relative military strengths allowed among the member nations.*

Q. What concentration camp near Munich was already in operation in the spring of 1933?

A. *Dachau. By the summer of that year many of Hitler's enemies were incarcerated there following the outlawing of all other political parties.*

Q. Who was killed on the Night of the Long Knives, June 30, 1934?

A. *Ernst Röhm, one of Hitler's old political comrades, who was now head of the Storm Troopers (the SA), which he wanted to unite with the regular army under his personal command. Hitler regarded that as being a threat to his own power and had Röhm and others dispatched by his personal security force.*

Q. What did Hitler proclaim himself in August of 1934?

1933–1939: Prologue to War

A. *Führer, following the death of President Hindenburg on August 2.*

Q. What did the Chinese Communists begin in October of 1934?

A. *The yearlong, six-thousand mile retreat that came to be called the Long March, undertaken to avoid being totally wiped out by Nationalist Chinese leader General Chiang Kai-shek. The Communists finally reestablished themselves at Yenan in north-central China.*

Q. The persecution of German Jews increased following Hitler's proclamation of the "Nuremberg Laws" in September of 1935. What did these "laws" do?

A. *They stripped Jews of their few remaining civil rights and set up gradations of Jewishness. Shortly after he became chancellor, Hitler had called for a boycott of all Jewish shops, and had subsequently gone on to remove Jews from all areas of public employment and to drive them out of both the medical and legal professions. But the persecution got even worse from 1935 on.*

Q. What did Leni Riefenstahl do at Nuremberg in September of 1934?

A. *She directed a documentary, at Hitler's request, of the huge annual Nazi rally held each year at the vast stadium designed by Albert Speer. The Nuremberg rallies were spectacles on a scale not seen since the fall of ancient Rome, and did much to bring the German people fully under Hitler's spell. Riefenstahl's film, called* Triumph of the Will, *is regarded as by far the most powerful propaganda film ever made. It was ravishing filmmaking and both fascinated and frightened viewers in Western Europe, Britain, and America. Riefenstahl went on to film the 1936 Berlin Olympics, producing a two-part hymn to the glories of the human body called Olympiad. Imprisoned for several years by the French after the war for her part in producing Nazi propaganda, she was never able to recover from her association with Hitler, and the accusation—always denied—that she was his mistress. There is no doubt, however, that her two major films were masterpieces of their kind.*

Q. In April of 1935, the U.S. Congress passed a bill that would tie President Roosevelt's hands in numerous ways during the first two years of the coming war in Europe. What was it called?

A. *The Neutrality Act. It made it unlawful for the United States to give financial assistance to any country involved in a war.*

Q. In June of 1935, an Anglo-German naval agreement was signed that not only violated the Treaty of Versailles signed after World War I, but also gave Germany a new opportunity to expand its military buildup. Under the agreement, Germany said that it would in no way contest British dominance of the seas, and in return, it would be allowed to have a navy 35 percent as large as Britain's. Why was this a disastrous move on the part of the British?

A. *Because Germany had only a token navy at the time. By getting approval to have up to 35 percent of British naval forces, it had in fact gained permission to build a navy that didn't exist. Worse, submarines could be built under the agreement—a mistake that came close to causing the defeat of Britain once the war began.*

Q. What North African country did Italy invade in October of 1935?

A. *Abyssinia (Ethiopia). Britain and France protested but did little more than wring their hands. Even so, under the brave leadership of Emperor Haile Selassie, the Abyssinians held out for six months.*

Q. What area that had been turned into a demilitarized zone after World War I did Hitler order German troops to occupy in early March of 1936?

A. *The Rhineland. Hitler's generals were dead set against this move, believing that their forces were not ready for a real fight, which is what they expected to get from the French in reaction to this move. But the French did little but let out a loud wail, and Hitler's success became a first step in his gradual domination of the German military.*

Q. To whose aid did the fascist governments of Italy and Germany come in 1936?

A. *Generalissimo Francisco Franco, in the Spanish Civil War. To the subsequent frustration of Hitler and Mussolini, Franco managed to stay out of the coming European war, offering verbal sympathy but maintaining a policy of "non-belligerence." Franco played what many regard as the cagiest hand of any European leader in World War II.*

Q. In Germany, 1937 was a year in which Hitler was content to build his armed forces and economy, but by the end of the year he had made a definite decision to move into two neighboring countries. Which were they?

A. *Austria and Czechoslovakia.*

Q. In China, 1937 was a seesaw year for the Japanese. The populace at home was ambivalent about the continued costs of the battles in China and the top military leaders were more interested in dealing with the Soviet Union, whom they suspected of expansionist plans. But younger field generals were determined to expand the conquered holdings in China. More forces were poured into Shanghai and by December they had captured what major Chinese city?

A. *The Chinese Nationalist capital, Nanking. In the north of China they had also taken Peking and were continuing to advance through northeastern China.*

Q. Which of the two potential Nazi targets, Austria and Czechoslovakia, were the French and British most concerned about?

A. *Czechoslovakia. They felt there was little they could do about Austria because of its increasingly large numbers of Nazi party members. But France could not let Czechoslovakia be invaded without responding; to fail to do so would indicate that a treaty with France was worthless. If the French were drawn in, the British felt bound to assist in terms of their own self-interest in keeping France strong.*

Q. What did British Foreign Secretary Anthony Eden do in February of 1938?

A. *He resigned from the Cabinet of Prime Minister Neville Chamberlain over policy—toward Italy in particular, but toward Hitler as well. British politics had been in turmoil for several years. A coalition government headed by Labour-*

ite Ramsay MacDonald had turned a blind eye to the rise of fascism. When the post of prime minister was assumed by Conservative Stanley Baldwin in 1935, he was quickly faced with a constitutional crisis over Edward VIII's insistence on marrying the American divorcee Wallis Simpson. Baldwin managed to force Edward to abdicate in favor of his younger brother, who became George VI, but in the wake of that extremely controversial episode and Baldwin's reluctance to challenge Hitler, Chamberlain took over in May of 1937. He too was waffling, and Eden was far more in tune with Winston Churchill, who was ostracized on the back benches but who continued at every opportunity to issue warnings of danger ahead.

Q. Italian physicist Enrico Fermi won the Nobel Prize in 1938. He went to Stockholm to accept, accompanied by his wife, and they continued straight on to New York. Why?

A. *His wife was Jewish, and anti-Semitic laws were being passed in Italy as well as Germany. Fermi was to become a crucial member of the team that developed the atomic bomb.*

Q. Austrian Nazis seized control of the government in early March of 1938 and German troops crossed into the country on the twelfth. What happened after Hitler's announcement that Austria was now a province of Nazi Germany?

A. *Following the pattern established when he came to power in Germany, known or potential opponents to Nazism were arrested by the tens of thousands.*

Q. On September 30, 1938, Neville Chamberlain waved a piece of paper in the air in front of 10 Downing Street and announced that it signified "peace in our time." What was this piece of paper?

A. *The agreement signed with Hitler in Munich. This infamous "solution" to the problem of Czechoslovakia, actually suggested by Chamberlain, called for the annexation by Germany of those areas of the country where more than 50 percent of the population approved of the move. This meant that Germany regained control of Sudetenland, with a population of nearly 3 million Sudetenese Germans as well as 800,000 Czechs. This was the most highly industrialized part of Czechoslovakia, and gave Germany 11,000 square miles of territory rich in coal, iron, and timber. The dismemberment of Czechoslovakia continued over the next six weeks, with Poland and Hungary also getting substantial chunks of the country.*

Q. In response to the Munich agreement, who said the following: "Britain and France had to choose between war and dishonor. They chose dishonor. They will have war."

A. *Winston Churchill.*

Q. Even in isolationist America, people were getting jumpy about what was happening in Europe. In various parts of the country, but especially in New Jersey and its neighboring states, there was panic on the night of October 30, 1938. Why?

A. *A radio broadcast of Orson Welles's extremely realistic adaptation of* The War of the Worlds *fed in to nervousness about potential war and led many people to believe that an invasion from Mars was actually taking place.*

Q. Why was the rampage against Jews in Germany on the ninth and tenth of November 1938 called "Kristallnacht" and what caused the attacks?

1933–1939: Prologue to War

A. *The name derived from the fact that the windows of at least 7,500 shops were broken and the stores looted. This was in reaction to the assassination of the third secretary of the German Embassy in Paris by a seventeen-year-old Jewish refugee whose father had been deported to Poland.*

Q. Chamberlain had his worthless piece of paper signed by Hitler. What country would sign a similar one in December 1938?

A. *France. This only gave Hitler another opportunity to say how peace-loving he was, even as he was demanding, and getting, a piece of Lithuania. By April he was demanding the return of Danzig to Germany, which not so incidentally would involve access to Lithuania through Poland.*

Q. In the United States, General George C. Marshall, who had been made Deputy Chief of Staff of the army only five months before, was promoted to Chief of Staff. How many officers with greater seniority were skipped over by Roosevelt in making this appointment?

A. *There were technically thirty-four officers in front of him. Roosevelt's early recognition of Marshall's great ability and intrinsic fairness and calm would serve the President in good stead for the next six years.*

Q. The Japanese had controlled all of China's main ports since the previous October, and thus had felt free to take on the Soviet Union in various incidents involving disputed borders. In May of 1939, one of these developed into a major confrontation that would last until mid-August. Which country prevailed?

A. *The Soviet Union. As a result, the Japanese backed off and turned their attention once again to consolidating their position in China.*

Q. As the hostilities began in May 1939 between the Japanese and the Russians, what were Germany and Italy concluding?

A. *A formal alliance known as "The Pact of Steel." Benito Mussolini had been in power far longer than Hitler, as prime minister since the end of 1922, and as dictator and head of the Fascist state since January of 1925. In 1934 he had even stood up to Hitler, unlike any of Europe's other leaders, by sending 50,000 troops to the Austrian border to forestall any attempt by Hitler to take over Austria following the assassination of Chancellor Dollfus, whose wife and children were actually visiting Mussolini at the time. But in the end he decided that it was wiser to be with Hitler than against him and had not intervened when Austria was finally annexed in 1938. "The Pact of Steel" simply ratified the new relationship.*

Q. The Germans and the Soviets signed a nonaggression pact on August 24, 1939. How many countries did they agree to divide up between them?

A. *Five—Poland, Lithuania, Finland, Estonia, and Latvia—although there were continuing revisions on who got how much of which country.*

Q. On August 31, 1939, Hitler made a broadcast announcing peace proposals directed at Poland. But these had not in fact been presented to Polish representatives. What did Hitler contrive that night?

1933–1939: Prologue to War

A. *The Germans simulated fake attacks on their own outposts on the Polish border, so that Hitler could claim Poland had started a war.*

Q. At dawn on September 1, 1939, fifty-three German divisions began smashing into Poland. How many divisions did the Polish have to counter the attack?

    a.   Two-thirds as many
    b.   Half as many
    c.   One-third as many

A. *They had half as many, including units being mobilized, and their armaments and planes were outdated.*

Q. Having signed a guarantee the previous year to protect Poland, what did the British and French do in the next twenty-four hours?

A. *Dithered frantically. Finally they sent Germany ultimatums to withdraw, which went unanswered. Prime Minister Chamberlain declared war on Germany on the third, as did Australia and New Zealand. The French quickly followed suit.*

Q. On September 3, 1939, a message was sent to all ships in the British Fleet saying, "Winston is back." What did this mean?

A. *Chamberlain had assembled a new War Cabinet, bringing in Anthony Eden as secretary of the dominions and Churchill as first lord of the admiralty. He had first served in that position beginning in 1911 and had been responsible for making the British Navy the finest in the world before the outbreak of World War I. Despite the several Cabinet posts he had held since, it was his first as overseer of the Royal Navy that was best remembered, and the navy could not have been happier to have him back. Long out of favor, he had not held a Cabinet post since 1929, but his hour had come again, and then some.*

Q. What did the United States declare on September 5, 1939?

A. *Its neutrality. Under the Neutrality Laws, Roosevelt had no choice.*

Q. What system to protect its shipping did Britain quickly establish?

A. *A convoy system, which had first been used in World War I, involving as few as five merchant vessels or up to five times that number, protected by armed escort ships of the navy. The senior naval officer was in command of the entire convoy. But even with this system, losses would be heavy for a long time to come because of the production of German submarines (U-boats) that had been allowed under the ill-advised Anglo-German naval agreement of 1935.*

Q. How long after the German invasion began did the Polish government leave Warsaw?

A. *Six days. Despite brave resistance on many fronts, the better-trained and -equipped German Army was simply slicing through Poland.*

Q. What crucial new blow hit Poland on September 17, 1939?

1933–1939: Prologue to War

A. *The Soviet Army invaded Poland from the east. Within ten days it was over, concluding with forty-eight hours of heavy German bombardment and air attacks on Warsaw. On the twenty-ninth, Germany and the Soviet Union agreed to partition the country.*

Q. How many Polish prisoners did the Germans and Soviets take between them?

A. *At least 900,000, with more than two thirds of them in German hands. Sufficient numbers of Poles escaped, however, to be able to form Free Polish divisions that would fight on numerous fronts in the course of the war.*

Q. With more than half of Poland in its hands (although the Nazis controlled the industrial west), the Soviet Union made demands for land concessions from what other country?

A. *Finland. The Soviet object was to establish a better position in the Baltic Sea. Negotiations would continue for nearly two months.*

Q. Who denounced Winston Churchill as a warmonger on October 6, 1939?

A. *Hitler, who claimed that all he had done was to redress the punitive measures of the Versailles Treaty of 1919.*

Q. What was established at Lublin in Poland in mid-October 1939?

A. *The first Jewish ghetto.*

Q. The British and French governments were both relieved by a modification made by the U.S. Congress in early November 1939. What was it?

A. *The Neutrality Laws were changed to make it possible to purchase arms from private U.S. companies for hard cash. But they were still sufficiently restrictive that Roosevelt would have to undertake some imaginative ploys to give the Allied forces, the British in particular, urgently needed help over the next year.*

Q. How soon did Hitler want to make an attack on the Low Countries, followed by a sweep into France?

A. *It had originally been scheduled for mid-November 1939, which appalled the German General Staff. Many officers had been worried that the French might attack Germany while the vast majority of German forces were tied up in Poland. Hitler did not believe that would happen, and the head of the Luftwaffe, Hermann Göring, backed Hitler up with his dismissal of the strength of the French air capability. Even so, the planned attack on Western Europe was repeatedly postponed through a combination of military objections and bad weather.*

Q. The series of fortified French bunkers known as the Maginot Line was one reason why the French did not attack Germany. It was believed that this nearly 200 miles of armed concrete could not be breached; thus it seemed foolish to expose French troops to battles in Germany, which would mean passing through its own Siegfried Line of similar but lesser fortifications. The Germans could not get into France, it was assumed, so why not just stay put. How formidable was the Maginot Line in reality?

1933–1939: Prologue to War

A. *Built at the then astronomical cost of $200 million over a period lasting from 1930 to 1937, and named for the Defense Minister André Maginot who presided over the planning for it, these fortifications were the last word in static defense. Living quarters were as deep as 100 feet underground and protected by 10-foot-thick concrete-sheathed artillery bunkers, forward pillboxes that were protected by barbed wire and tank traps. The fortifications were so placed that their guns could cover any ground that lay between them. There was only one problem—the Belgians had refused to have any built on their territory, making the end run Hitler planned possible.*

Q. Unaware of what Hitler was planning, the wary but not altogether cooperative Western European nations and Britain were distracted by the beginning of what conflict on November 30, 1939?

A. *The war between Finland and the Soviet Union. The Finnish government had seemed for the past two months to regard the Soviet threats as a bluff, and then realized too late that they were not. There is considerable evidence that the Allied nations of Western Europe underrated Soviet military power. It was known, at least to some extent, that Stalin had carried out purges of the Soviet Army in 1937, and that led to an assumption of a considerably weakened force. The Soviet invasion of Poland was being discounted because it had followed the German invasion by nearly three weeks. And little attention had been paid to General Georgi Zhukov's thorough thrashing of the Japanese at the end of August of that year. The valiant Finnish resistance to the Soviet attack only added to the impression, as the two countries offset one another's victories through December.*

Q. First Lord of the Admiralty Winston Churchill and the Royal Navy he commanded did not have time to be distracted, however. There were the transatlantic convoys to protect from an ever-increasing number of German U-boats. And there was also the matter of the *Graf Spee* to be dealt with. What was the *Graf Spee*?

A. *The* Graf Spee *was what was known as a "pocket battleship," one of several small but fast and heavily armed German ships that acted as marauders against merchant shipping, picking off unescorted vessels that were out of the operational field of the U-boats at that time. The* Graf Spee *had been especially successful at this kind of attack, operating principally in the South Atlantic.*

Q. Where did the British corner the *Graf Spee*?

A. *Damaged off Uruguay by three British cruisers, the* Graf Spee *took refuge in the harbor at Montevideo. Although the British cruisers had all been damaged as well, British diplomats in Montevideo managed to create the impression that a fresh force was already in position. Captain Hans Langsdorff decided to scuttle the* Graf Spee *rather than fight a useless battle that would only result in the deaths of his crew. On December 17, 1939, the ship was blown up just off the coast by its own crew, with thousands watching from the shore. Three days later, realizing that he had been duped, Captain Langsdorff committed suicide. Hitler did not tolerate surrender or withdrawal, and Langsdorff would be only one of countless suicides Hitler would ordain, one way or another, in the long ghastly years to come.*

Part Two
1940: Europe Under the Blitzkrieg

Q. In a portent of things to come, three of the most cherished of British foodstuffs were first rationed on January 8, 1940. What were they?

A. *Bacon, butter, and sugar.*

Q. Hitler had planned to begin an invasion of Western Europe on January 17. What caused him to delay?

    a.   German generals were against it
    b.   German plans fell into Allied hands
    c.   Hitler wanted to await the outcome of the Soviet-Finnish war

A. *German plans fell into Allied hands when a German plane went off course and was forced down in Belgium. To the relief of at least some officers, Hitler delayed the attack until spring.*

Q. In what theater of war did the Germans score large successes in January of 1940?

A. *At sea, where German submarines sank forty Allied vessels. The U-boats were particularly successful in the North Sea.*

Q. On February 1, a new Japanese budget was passed. How much of it was given over to military development?

    a. One quarter
    b. Over a third
    c. Almost half

A. *The answer is* c, *a cause for alarm in Washington.*

Q. When the British announced on February 14 that all British merchant ships operating in the North Sea would henceforth be armed, what was Germany's response?

A. *Germany said that they would therefore regard them as ships of war, but since Germany was sinking them anyway, it was hardly a change in policy. It was typical of Hitler to behave as though he had previously regarded the merchant ships as innocent bystanders.*

Q. Also on the fourteenth, the German transport *Altmart* entered Norwegian territorial waters. On board were 299 British sailors who had been transferred from the *Graf Spee* before it was scuttled. Since his ship was now in supposedly neutral waters, what should the captain of the *Altmart* have done?

A. *Under international law he should have released them. When he did not, the crew of a British destroyer boarded and took them off, also a violation of international law. Hitler was infuriated and became further convinced of the need to invade Norway.*

Q. The Germans began a major construction project near a small Polish town in the third week of February. This virtually

30

unheard-of town would subsequently become infamous. What was the name of the town and what was being constructed?

A. *Auschwitz had been chosen as the site of a huge concentration camp.*

Q. After three and a half months of battle, an armistice was signed between what two countries on March 13?

A. *Finland and the Soviet Union. The armistice required Finland to cede the strategic Karelian Isthmus to the USSR.*

Q. During the Finnish-Soviet War, the Finns had only 200,000 troops at best, and lost 25,000 men with more than 45,000 wounded. Yet the Soviet Union, with six times as many troops, nevertheless had almost twice as many dead and more than three times as many wounded. What did both Hitler and Allied leaders take this to mean?

A. *That the Soviet Union would be vulnerable to German invasion.*

Q. The word *quisling,* meaning "traitor," came into the English language in the spring of 1940. From what does it derive?

A. *Hitler's army invaded Denmark and Norway on April 4, 1940. The Norwegian politician Vidkun Quisling, a Nazi sympathizer, helped to facilitate the invasion of Norway and was ultimately rewarded by being made its puppet ruler in 1941.*

Q. Why had neither Denmark nor Norway expected to be invaded?

A. *Both countries had declared their neutrality. But convinced by the* Altmark *incident in February that the British would interfere in Norway, Hitler decided to secure it and to take Denmark in the process.*

Q. How long did Denmark hold out?

A. *Totally unprepared for war and under threat of having Copenhagen bombed, Denmark surrendered on April 9.*

Q. Norway, however, resisted strongly and, with the aid of British and French troops, was able to give the Germans real trouble. How long was it before Norway fell?

A. *The Allies withdrew from central Norway on May 2, but were able to hold the mountains until June.*

Q. By May, there were thirteen British divisions in France to aid in that country's defense. How well prepared were they?

A. *Only half were well trained and equipped. The rest were hastily assembled and full of volunteers who, though charged with spirit, were essentially amateurs.*

Q. On May 10, Germany invaded Holland, Belgium, and Luxembourg. But on the same day an event of far-reaching importance occurred in England. What was it?

A. *Winston Churchill was called upon to become prime minister, replacing the discredited Neville Chamberlain.*

Q. On the eleventh, British and French troops landed on the Dutch-held islands of Aruba and Curaçao in the Caribbean. Why?

1940: Europe Under the Blitzkrieg

A. *To secure the oil refineries on the islands and protect the sea-lanes to oil-rich Venezuela.*

Q. As the Germans began to invade France on the twelfth, what did Churchill offer the British people in a radio broadcast?

A. *Nothing but "blood, toil, tears, and sweat."*

Q. What queen and her family were evacuated to London from the Continent on May 13?

A. *Queen Wilhelmina of the Netherlands. Members of the Dutch government were also transported to London, and the country surrendered to the Germans the next day.*

Q. On the fifteenth, President Roosevelt received the first of many telegrams signed "Former Naval Person." Who was this person?

A. *Prime Minister Churchill.*

Q. A hero of the First World War was made deputy prime minister of France in a reorganization of Prime Minister Paul Reynaud's government on May 18. Name him.

A. *Marshal Henri Pétain.*

Q. Despite heavy resistance from Belgian, French, and British troops, the German army had established a twenty-mile-wide corridor to what by May 20?

A. *The English Channel, thus putting Allied troops farther up the coast at risk.*

Q. As the Allied troops were continually pushed back by the Germans, the British plan called Operation Dynamo was put into effect on May 26. What was this plan?

A. *To evacuate British and Allied troops across the Channel. Dunkirk, the major port in northern France, was chosen as the point of evacuation.*

Q. When the plans for Operation Dynamo were drawn up, how many troops did the British expect to be able to evacuate?

    a.   50,000
    b.   100,000
    c.   200,000

A. *The planners did not believe there would be time to get more than 50,000 back across the Channel to England.*

Q. With France falling, how well was the Marginot Line holding up?

A. *Only one section of blockhouses was captured by the Germans in actual fighting. But by going around it through Belgium, the Germans were able simply to roll through France. Tank commander General Erwin Rommel wrote to his wife from Rennes, "Reached here without difficulty. The war has become practically a lightning Tour de France."*

Q. The evacuation of Allied troops and resistance fighters from Dunkirk that began on May 26 lasted until June 4. Which of the following declared the operation a "nine days' wonder"?

    a.   Prime Minister Churchill
    b.   Poet Laureate John Masefield
    c.   King George VI

1940: Europe Under the Blitzkrieg

A. *John Masefield. Churchill called it a "miracle of deliverance."*

Q. Despite air attacks by the Germans, the flotilla of boats ranging from destroyers to fishing boats was able to rescue how many men from Dunkirk?

    a. 200,000
    b. 275,000
    c. 340,000

A. *The answer is c, with 200,000 of those being British, 110,000 French, and the rest Belgians and Poles. The French soldiers were mostly shipped back across the Channel to France to aid in the continuing struggle in their own country.*

Q. How many Allied troops were left in Dunkirk when the Germans closed in on the port?

A. *About 40,000, mostly French soldiers, were captured.*

Q. How many Royal Air Force pilots were lost protecting the Dunkirk rescue ships from Luftwaffe planes?

    a. 40
    b. 80
    c. 100

A. *The answer is b. Eighty merchant ships and smaller warships, and six destroyers, were also lost.*

Q. Another evacuation of troops from the Continent took place June 4 through 8. Where did this occur?

A. *Norway, from which 24,000 troops were withdrawn.*

Q. On June 5, a newly promoted general was made the French under secretary for defense. Name him.

A. *Charles de Gaulle.*

Q. Who declared war on Britain and France on June 10?

A. *Mussolini, who was feeling left out.*

Q. On June 13, the United States dispatched a shipment of small arms to Britain. Why did the government first sell them to a steel company, which then resold them to the British government?

A. *In order to get around the U.S. Neutrality Laws.*

Q. Paris was occupied by the Nazis on June 14. How fierce was the fighting?

A. *There was no defense, with hardly a shot fired.*

Q. What three small independent countries did the Soviet Union occupy on June 15?

A. *Lithuania, Latvia, and Estonia.*

Q. Hitler ordered that the surrender of France on June 22 take place in the small town of Rethondes in eastern France. Why was this location so important to him?

1940: Europe Under the Blitzkrieg

A. *Hitler was photographed dancing a small jig of joy at Rethondes, because this was the very spot on which Germany had surrendered to France at the end of World War I, twenty-two years earlier. He even had the same railway carriage in which the previous surrender had been signed brought to Rethondes.*

Q. Marshal Pétain, then eighty-four years old, was called on to form a government following the despairing resignation of Paul Reynaud on June 16. Great hero of the First World War though he was, Pétain had never believed that France could withstand Hitler's advance, and was convinced that Britain also would fall. His objective was to preserve as much of the autonomy of France as possible. On July 1 the Pétain government established headquarters at Vichy (home of the mineral water) in central France. Why didn't Pétain run his government from Paris?

A. *Under the armistice agreement with Germany, 60 percent of France, including Paris, was controlled and occupied by the Nazis. The remainder was supposedly under the control of the Pétain government, but it included only the weakest areas economically and the Germans in fact operated as they pleased even here. To run an even slightly "autonomous" France from a backwater like Vichy was a contradiction in terms.*

Q. Whom did the British recognize as the "head of all free France" on June 28?

A. *Charles de Gaulle, who had fled to London on June 17, where he made two famous broadcasts on the eighteenth and nineteenth vowing to sustain the honor of France and to resist the Nazis until France's sovereignty was restored, calling for a volunteer force to join with him.*

Q. Did the fall of France greatly influence American public opinion concerning the war in Europe?

A. *Yes. A Gallup poll on June 2 had shown Americans to be almost equally divided on whether the United States should even go so far as to offer economic aid to Britain and the Allies. After the fall of France, support for such aid rose to 67 percent.*

Q. What was the main reason Roosevelt broke with tradition and ran for a third term as president?

A. *The isolationist feeling in the country was so strong that he did not feel any of the potential candidates in either party would be able to steer a course that would prepare the country for a war he felt was in the long run inevitable. As the June 2 Gallup poll showed, the country as a whole was extremely ambivalent about any involvement in the European struggle, and the isolationist voices were much the loudest. At the end of May, the Republican party had nominated a nonpolitician, the business leader Wendell L. Willkie, a former Roosevelt supporter who had broken with the president because he was so strongly against getting involved in the European conflict. After the fall of France, it was possible to get new military procurement bills through Congress, but the isolationists were at full shout throughout the presidential campaign.*

Q. During the almost daily bombardment of the British island of Malta in the Mediterranean during June of 1940, the nicknames Faith, Hope, and Charity were given to what?

A. *The three Gladiator fighter airplanes that remained to try to defend the island from German attack.*

Q. The fleet of what country was bombed at Mers-el-Kebir, Algeria, by the British on July 3, 1940?

1940: Europe Under the Blitzkrieg

A. *The French fleet. Now that France was under the control of Germany, its fleet had to be considered part of the enemy arsenal.*

Q. German successes in the summer of 1940 emboldened Mussolini to take aggressive steps of his own. Connect the Italian action in the left-hand column with the correct date in the right-hand column.

1.	Italy declares war on Britain and France	a.	August 5
2.	Italy invades Egypt	b.	June 10
3.	Italy invades British Somaliland	c.	September 13

A. *1,b; 2,a; 3,c.*

Q. The Battle of Britain opened on July 10, 1940, with the bombing of British coastal towns from Plymouth to Dover. At this point, the Luftwaffe had 10,000 fully trained pilots. How many did the Royal Air Force have?

a. 1,450
b. 2,700
c. 3,400

A. *The answer is a, and the British were training new pilots at the rate of only 50 a month.*

Q. Was Germany or Great Britain turning out new planes at a faster rate in July of 1940?

A. *Here the British had the advantage. They were manufacturing 500 Vickers Spitfires and Hawker Hurricanes a month, while the Germans were turning out only 230 Messerschmitt Me-109s and Me-110s.*

Q. The British also had the advantage of operating from their home base, which meant that more men and planes could be saved when a plane was hit during battle, while the Germans had to fly 120 miles back across the Channel. But the greatest British advantage was a new technology that RAF Chief Marshal Sir Hugh Dowding had begun championing in the mid-thirties. What was it?

A. *Radar. Thanks to the foresight of Dowding, the British were the world leaders in the development of radar defenses.*

Q. What is the word radar an abbreviation of?

A. *RAdio-Detection-And-Ranging device.*

Q. The electronic impulses of radar travel outward at what speed?
   a. 93,000 miles per second
   b. 152,000 miles per second
   c. 186,000 miles per second

A. *They travel outward at 186,000 miles per second, the speed of light.*

Q. British radar installations proved crucial in the Battle of Britain. How many aircraft did the Germans have available for the attack on Britain?
   a. 2,500
   b. 3,500
   c. 4,000

A. *Germany had 3,500 aircraft, including 1,300 long-range bombers, 300 reconnaissance planes, 500 dive bombers, and 1,100 fighters, of which 350 were twin-engine planes.*

1940: Europe Under the Blitzkrieg

Q. During the summer of 1940, a U.S. senator from the "Show Me" state drove 25,000 miles in his own car inspecting defense plants after hundreds of complaints about inefficiency were lodged with Congress. What was the senator's name?

A. *Harry S Truman, who returned to Washington and demanded the creation of a special oversight committee. The Special Committee to Investigate the National Defense Program was set up by Congress that fall. Truman served as its chairman until he ran for the vice-presidency in 1944.*

Q. Why didn't Truman use a period after the *S* in his name?

A. *Because he had no actual middle name; as he himself put it, it was "S for nothing."*

Q. On July 25, 1940, a week after Roosevelt's renomination, the United States placed an embargo on the shipment of strategic materials to what country?

A. *Japan. Concern about the Japanese military buildup had been growing in Washington for some time. Renominated, Roosevelt felt he could take this step that the isolationists regarded as "asking for trouble."*

Q. On September 2, 1940, the United States gave Britain fifty World War I destroyers. Under the Neutrality Laws, this was not legal. But the United States got something in return that made the deal difficult for even isolationists to criticize. What did the United States get?

A. *The British gave the United States the right to establish bases in the West Indies and on Bermuda. One isolationist*

*senator regretted Roosevelt's cleverness, saying that oppos-
ing the deal would be like opposing the Louisiana Purchase.*

Q. What unique defensive measure narrowly passed Congress
in September?

A. *The first peacetime draft in U.S. history.*

Q. The draft had a misleading name attached to it. What was it?

A. *It was called the Selective Training and Service Bill. By
emphasizing the "training" aspect of the measure,
Roosevelt was attempting to soft-pedal the possibility of actual fighting. Isolationists predicted draft riots, but 16 million men would register without incident on October 16, and
the first numbers would be drawn on October 29, using the
same huge glass bowl that had been drawn from to inaugu-
rate the wartime draft of 1917.*

Q. Why didn't Hitler order air attacks against London sooner
than September 7, 1940?

A. *He had continued to believe that he could force the British
to sign a peace treaty with Germany, on Germany's terms,
and did not want to make it more difficult for Churchill to
give in.*

Q. On September 10, a bomb hit Buckingham Palace. The
Royal Family was in residence, but having narrowly escaped
injury, expressed relief that the palace had been hit. Why?

A. *The first three days of bombing had been concentrated on
East London, the area of docks and factories where the*

Cockneys lived. London's poorest people were thus taking the brunt of the attack. When the palace was hit, government censors banned the story from the newspapers. Churchill called them "stupid fools" and ordered the news printed. Both he and the Royal Family felt that it was important that it be understood that everyone was in this together, no matter what their status.

Q. On September 22, Vichy France—as it had come to be called in contrast to de Gaulle's concept of the resistance of those dedicated to Free France—agreed to allow Japan to establish air bases in what area long under French control?

A. *Indochina. Japan joined the Tripartite Alliance with Germany and Italy five days later.*

Q. What were Enigma machines?

A. *The German code machines for sending orders. The British cracked the code early in the war, and established separate Service Units (SUs) for the navy, the army, and the air force. These units monitored all enemy air traffic.*

Q. What were barrage balloons?

A. *These were large helium-filled balloons with long metal cables hanging beneath them. They were released by the British during air attacks. Floating high above the coast they were surprisingly successful at damaging German planes that got entangled in the cables. Some Luftwaffe planes were equipped with "bumpers" at the front of the plane, which consisted of outward-facing triangles of metal that could push the cables to either side. But the bumpers were so heavy that they cut down on speed and increased fuel consumption.*

Q. What unlikely site was equipped with 6,000 bunks, a children's playroom, and a library, and offered dance instruction?

A. *The Liverpool stop of London's Underground (subway), which was one of the stations most heavily used as a bomb shelter. Such amenities were not put in place until 1941, nor was the use of the Underground stations even officially approved at first, but people fled to them as the Battle of Britain got under way.*

Q. One of the most highly regarded RAF pilots was Douglas Boder, the squadron leader of the wing based in Dufford, England. It was remarkable that he was flying at all. Why?

A. *He had tin legs, having lost his own in a 1931 accident.*

Q. What was the Eagle Squadron?

A. *There were eventually two Eagle Squadrons, made up of Americans trained in Canada. They wore RAF uniforms with an Eagle patch. After America entered the European war in 1942, they were transferred to American command, but a few pilots were granted their wish to continue flying with the RAF.*

Q. Germany's Junker-87 dive bombers had proved very successful during the Battle of France. Did they hold up well in the Battle of Britain?

1940: Europe Under the Blitzkrieg

A. *No. Against British fighters they turned out to be extremely vulnerable at the moment when they slowed to pull out of a dive. So many were lost that they were withdrawn from use over the Channel on August 16.*

Q. During the blitz of London, groups of men spent night after night sleeping in the chapel of St. Paul's Cathedral. Why?

A. *They were volunteer firemen, who wanted to be on the actual scene if this greatly revered edifice were to be hit by a bomb. Although the area around the cathedral was demolished, St. Paul's itself escaped with only secondary damage.*

Q. The Battle of Britain came to an end on October 31, when Hitler decided that it was not going to be possible to bomb England sufficiently to make a sea invasion viable. From July 10 to October 31 the RAF lost 915 aircraft. How many Luftwaffe planes did it bring down?

    a.   1,733
    b.   2,104
    c.   2,698

A. *The British believed at the time they had brought down 2,698 German planes, but after the war German records were found to list only 1,733 losses. Whatever the number, it was enough to end Operation Sea Lion, as the Germans had code-named the invasion of Britain.*

Q. Had the Germans also overestimated the number of RAF planes shot down?

A. *Yes, and even more drastically. By September 5, Luftwaffe chief Hermann Göring believed that the British had only*

45

100 planes left. This miscalculation led to even heavier losses for the Luftwaffe over the next weeks, and had its effect on Hitler's decision to call off the invasion.

Q. To this day, the RAF pilots who fought the Battle of Britain are known as The Few. How did they get this name?

A. *It came from Churchill's famous statement: "Never in the field of human conflict was so much owed by so many to so few."*

Q. After the Battle of Britain, did Germany stop bombing London?

A. *No. Night bombing of London continued throughout the war, but it was never as concentrated as during the Battle of Britain, and there were no major raids from mid-1941 to 1944. The Luftwaffe was too busy laying waste to other parts of the country.*

Q. Changing strategy, Germany decided to attack the industrial towns of the English Midlands. From 8:15 P.M. on November 14 to dawn the next morning, they dropped 50 tons of incendiary bombs and 394 tons of high-explosive bombs on what famous cathedral town?

A. *Coventry. Twelve aircraft factories and nine other manufacturing plants were damaged and the fourteenth-century cathedral was reduced to rubble. After the war, the ruins of the old cathedral were incorporated in the structure of a new one.*

Q. Germany was at the same time consolidating its power to the east. Name the two adjacent countries bordering on the

Soviet Union that joined the Axis alliance on November 20 and 22.

A. *Hungary and Romania, neither of which had the slightest choice in the matter by this time. German troops had entered Romania six weeks before.*

Q. Franklin D. Roosevelt's election to a third term was by a smaller electoral margin than his landslide victory of 1936. How many electoral votes did his opponent Wendell Willkie amass?

    a.   65
    b.   82
    c.   123

A. *Willkie got 82 electoral votes to Roosevelt's 449. This was five less than Herbert Hoover got in 1932 but a lot more than Alfred Landon's paltry 8 electoral votes in 1936.*

Q. From the British aircraft carrier *Illustrious,* a bombing attack was launched on November 11 that did great damage to the Italian fleet at Taranto naval base. This brilliant strategic success was scrutinized with particular care by what country?

A. *Japan.*

Q. The British had another airborne success on the nineteenth of November. In the Atlantic, a Sunderland flying boat used new technology to spot a U-boat shadowing a convoy. What was this new technology?

A. *Improved radar that was situated in the nose cone. This was the first time radar had been used in this way. The Sunder-*

47

*land flying boats proved extremely valuable throughout the
war. With a range of 2,880 miles over a thirteen-and-a-half
hour flying time, and armed with machine guns, depth
charges, and antisubmarine bombs, they proved so damaging that the Germans called them "Flying Porcupines."*

Q. In late November, the Nazis began another of their nefarious
construction projects in Poland. This one was in Warsaw.
What was it?

A. *The Warsaw Ghetto, in which all Jews would be confined for
what the Nazis called "reasons of health."*

Q. On December 7, two British divisions began a march from
Mersa Matruh in North Africa. What was their objective?

A. *To drive the Italian army out of Egypt. Three days later the
British reached the Italian front and captured two Italian
camps.*

Q. On the thirteenth of December, Hitler issued a directive
concerning the planned spring invasion of Greece, called
Operation Marita. What did this plan make clear about Hitler's attitude toward its Axis partner Italy?

A. *It made clear that Hitler was not going to allow Italy to be
the sole occupier of any country. Italy had already begun an
invasion of Greece at the end of October. This step had been
taken by Mussolini without consulting Hitler, and the Führer was still angry about it, although he was careful to hide
the fact from Mussolini.*

Q. On December 17, Roosevelt first discussed a new concept
that he compared to lending a neighbor a hose to help put out

a fire at his house, noting that this loan would help make sure that the flames did not spread to his own property. What did this program to help Britain come to be called?

A. *Lend-Lease. Formally introduced to Congress on January 10, 1941, it allowed the British to buy food and raw materials from the United States without paying for them until the war was over. Initially, the bill met with heavy opposition from isolationist members of Congress, but was championed by Henry Stimson, the Republican whom Roosevelt had appointed secretary of war in June of 1940. The bill passed on March 11, 1941. Lend-Lease has been called one of the most generous acts ever made by one nation to another.*

Part Three
1941: World War

Q. What happened at manufacturing plants in or near Seattle, Washington; Long Beach, California; Niagara Falls, New York; and Marietta, Georgia, early in 1941?

A. *The Boeing, Douglas, and Bell aircraft companies began building new military planes for the government.*

Q. On January 2, Roosevelt announced a program for the building of two hundred freighters of identical design. What were the ships to be called?

A. *Liberty Ships.*

Q. Why did Roosevelt use the phrase "arsenal of democracy" to refer to the United States in his January 6 State of the Union speech?

A. *It was a phrase Roosevelt had used before and would use several times again because he felt it carried a subtle message that the United States must be prepared for war.*

Q. On January 10, 1941, Germany and the Soviet Union signed agreements concerning frontiers in Eastern Europe and the trade of food and industrial equipment. Did Hitler intend to honor these agreements?

A. *No. He had already hatched plans in December for the invasion of the Soviet Union, an operation code-named Barbarossa.*

Q. In mid-January, the Germans and Italians both attacked the island of Malta from the air. The British carrier *Illustrious* was damaged on both the sixteenth and the nineteenth, and British airfields were hit on the eighteenth. What was the main reason Malta would be steadily under attack for the rest of 1941 and beyond?

A. *It was crucially located for supplying Allied forces in North Africa, as well as for disrupting the flow of German and Italian supplies in the same region. But although its people suffered greatly, it was also very heavily defended. Throughout history, the island had been a strategic must in controlling the Mediterranean Sea.*

Q. The British had great success, under the leadership of the Commander of the Middle East (which included North Africa), General Sir Archibald Wavell, against the Italians in January and February. They captured 17,000 Italian troops in Sudan on January 19 and another 25,000 at Beda Fomm in Libya on February 7. Why were the Italians so easily demoralized in these battles?

A. *Aside from being badly led, many of them were essentially occupying troops, unused to battle and tired of the desert areas that Italy had controlled for several years.*

Q. The Regent of Yugoslavia, Prince Paul, signed an agreement with Germany to join the Axis alliance on March 25. What happened to Prince Paul the next day?

1941: World War

A. *He was overturned in a coup, and King Peter II, only seventeen years old, was installed in his place, but the real power was put in the hands of Air Force Chief of Staff, General Simovic.*

Q. The prime minister of Hungary, Count Teleki, did what rather than cooperate with the Nazis?

A. *Committed suicide on April 2.*

Q. In late March the British battleship *Malaya* had been damaged by German torpedoes in the Atlantic. What did Roosevelt allow the ship to do in early April?

A. *The battleship was allowed to put in at New York harbor for repairs. This was the first time a British warship had been given clearance for such a docking; neutrality was continuing to be eroded, little by little.*

Q. On February 8, Germany and Bulgaria signed a military pact. Of what particular strategic importance was this pact to Hitler?

A. *It meant that German troops would be allowed to pass through Bulgaria to attack its immediate neighbor, Greece.*

Q. The pact with Bulgaria persuaded Churchill to agree to send British troops to assist Greece. Greece had been asking for such help for nearly a month before it was granted on February 10. Why was Churchill so reluctant to offer it?

A. *Because it meant withdrawing troops from Africa and transferring them to Greece.*

Q. The arrival of this German officer in Tripoli on February 12 portended a new phase in the battle for control of North Africa. Name the officer.

A. *General Erwin Rommel.*

Q. In the third week of February, Foreign Minister Anthony Eden and British military commanders met in Athens with King George of Greece to discuss the defense of that country. How many British troops was it agreed would be needed?

  a. 50,000
  b. 75,000
  c. 100,000

A. *It was agreed that any fewer than 100,000 men would be unable to do the job.*

Q. Starting in March, the British had considerable success against German U-boats, including the sinking of three boats whose captains were particular favorites of Hitler. Why was this especially gratifying to Churchill?

A. *After the war, Churchill would say, "The only thing that ever really frightened me during the war was the U-boat peril."*

Q. The capture of the submarine *U-110* carried special significance because of the presence on board of what kind of equipment?

A. *An intact coding machine, which enabled the British to break the German naval code.*

Q. On March 12, a month after his arrival in Africa, Rommel held a military parade in the central square of Tripoli with the aim of impressing the largely Italian population and with the expectation that news of the strength of his Afrika Korps would get back to the British. In fact, the major part of his troops and tanks had yet to arrive. But it seemed as though an endless stream of tanks was passing his reviewing stand. How did he achieve this?

A. *After a tank had passed through it would make a large circle through the back streets and come through again.*

Q. Rommel attacked the British-held town of El Agheila. The British, feeling that they could not withstand as large a force as Rommel commanded, retreated. Is it true or false that a significant number of Rommel's tanks were in fact fakes?

A. *It is true. He had tanks constructed in Tripoli of cardboard and canvas, which he then mounted on Volkswagen chassis. From the air, the dust created by the column obscured the fake tanks, fooling the British.*

Q. Who gave Rommel the nickname "The Desert Fox"?

A. *British troops. The British in general respected Rommel more than any other wartime opponent since Napoleon.*

Q. Was the German high command pleased with Rommel's progress in the western desert in March of 1941?

A. *No. Five days before he attacked El Agheila, he had been flown to Berlin, where he was told to stay put and await reinforcements before making any attacks. Rommel, however, knew that the British had withdrawn forces from North*

57

Africa to defend Greece and wanted to attack while they were undermanned.

Q. Rommel continued on the attack, targeting the next British position between himself and Tobruk, Mersa Briga. Again the British retreated. In the course of that retreat what happened to the British generals Neame and O'Conner?

A. *The driver of the staff car they were traveling in together got lost in the desert and drove straight into a German-occupied town. The generals were captured and held in Italy as prisoners of war for the next three years.*

Q. Did any of Rommel's forces ever get lost in the desert?

A. *Yes. On one occasion, Rommel went searching by plane for a group of lost tanks. He thought he had found them and was preparing to land when at the last moment he saw that they were British forces. His plane was hit by machine-gun fire but he was able to escape.*

Q. Although the British were retreating in the western desert, they were having good success in another part of Africa. What capital held by the Italians since 1936 did the British occupy on April 6?

A. *Addis Ababa, capital of Ethiopia.*

Q. What two European countries did Germany invade on April 6?

A. *Yugoslavia and Greece.*

1941: World War

Q. On April 14 and 16, Rommel tried to take Tobruk from the Australians. Was he successful?

A. *No, he was beaten back. He was badly hampered by dust storms but the Australians were also fierce fighters. They had been told to hold Tobruk at all costs and their new commander, the Australian Major General Leslie Morshead was as tough as they came. By day the troops defended Tobruk; by night, they made harassing raids on the Germans.*

Q. Fighting in the desert was physically exhausting. Aside from the necessity of severely rationing water, and the dust storms that blew up out of nowhere, the temperature was the biggest problem. How much could the temperature vary in a single day?

A. *As much as sixty degrees. Lambasted by intense heat during the day, troops were often shivering at night.*

Q. In the United States in mid-April, Roosevelt quietly created a new executive department that would have enormous impact on the way Americans lived once the country entered the war. What was this office called?

A. *The Office of Price Administration, headed by Leon Henderson, which would control both the availability and price of all goods.*

Q. Also in mid-April, the Japanese and the Soviet Union signed a five-year nonaggression agreement. Why were both countries very eager to make this agreement?

A. *Japan didn't want to have to worry about its backdoor neighbor while it expanded in the South Pacific, and Stalin was increasingly suspicious of Hitler's plans, wanting to be able to use the troops on the Sea of Japan to defend against any possible attack from the west.*

Q. After the fall of Yugoslavia, Roman Catholic followers of the German puppet, Ante Pavelich, began to murder Orthodox Serbo-Croatians. How many people did they eventually kill?

    a.   100,000
    b.   250,000
    c.   500,000

A. *The answer is c. Even priests joined in the killing. As part of his deal with Hitler, Croatia was declared independent of Yugoslavia, giving Pavelich complete power.*

Q. It took the Germans an additional week to conquer Greece. To what island did King George and members of his government finally flee on the twenty-third of April?

A. *Crete.*

Q. On April 30, Rommel tried once more to take Tobruk, but this time the dust storms caused such havoc that his troops suffered heavy casualties, with the loss of over a thousand men. What was the reaction in Berlin?

A. *They sent a more senior general to get Rommel to stop trying to take Tobruk until more troops arrived.*

Q. This diminutive ruler with a reputation for bravery was able to return to the capital of his country on May 5. Name him.

A. *Emperor Haile Selassie of Ethiopia, who had personally led his subjects in defending against the Italian invasion in the mid-thirties, was finally able to return from his exile in England and retake his throne in Addis Ababa following the British defeat of the Italian occupying forces.*

Q. In one of the more bizarre incidents of the war, a high-ranking Nazi leader showed up in Scotland on May 10 on a personal "peace mission." Name him and describe his means of arrival.

A. *Rudolf Hess, one of Hitler's closest confidants, landed in Scotland by parachute. It has never been fully determined whether Hitler had ordered this stunt or whether Hess was operating on his own. However, Hess's argument that the British were, like the Germans, an Aryan people, and ought to be with Germany rather than against it, was certainly in line with Hitler's racial preoccupations. Since Germany was about to invade Russia, it also would have been advantageous to neutralize Britain at this point.*

Q. Germany invaded British-held Crete on May 20, in a manner that was a military first. What did the Germans do?

A. *They parachuted troops onto Crete, marking the first time in history an invasion had been made from the air.*

Q. In early April the British had seriously damaged the German cruiser *Gneisenau* on a bombing raid on the German facilities at Brest. The absence of the *Gneisenau* as a support vessel was very helpful to the British in a famous attack on a German battleship in the Denmark Strait on May 24. Name the German battleship that was attacked.

A. *The* Bismark, *Germany's largest battleship, was attacked by the British battleships* Hood *and* Prince of Wales. *In the ensuing battle, the* Hood's *magazine was hit and the ship blew up, with only three survivors out of nearly 1,500 men. But the* Bismark *was also badly damaged, and as it limped toward the French port of Saint-Nazaire, it was attacked by British planes and sunk on May 27. Only 110 out of 2,000 men survived.*

Q. Despite strong resistance, the Allied forces on Crete were losing ground steadily in the second week of May and it was necessary to evacuate King George of Greece from this supposed refuge. In what country did he arrive on May 23?

A. *Egypt. There was fighting going on in both East and North Africa, but Cairo was regarded as safe. It was becoming increasingly difficult to find any safe havens in Europe or the Middle East.*

Q. At the end of May, Allied forces were removed from Crete. The German paratroop invasion had succeeded brilliantly. Why then did Hitler decide not to use the technique again?

A. *Because German losses had been high, with large numbers of deaths. The taking of Crete had been, relatively speaking, extremely costly.*

Q. Because of its oil, Syria became a battleground in the second week of June, as British and Free French troops moved in. What opposing force was in control at that point?

A. *French Vichy forces, which were overcome by the fourteenth.*

Q. Tobruk had become a point of increasing concern for Churchill. It was surrounded by Rommel's forces, and it was very difficult to supply; this could be done only from the sea. British destroyers would slip into the harbor at night, but there was continual harassment from the Luftwaffe. Churchill thus ordered a major attack to dislodge Rommel. This land operation failed, however. What did Churchill's disappointment lead him to do?

A. *He replaced General Wavell, who had been one of his favorites, with General Sir Claude Auchinleck, the Commander in Chief in India. Wavell was sent to India in his stead. Wavell, worn out by his complex duties in overseeing the entire Mideast, including North Africa, felt that Churchill's decision was quite right.*

Q. What Middle Eastern country signed a friendship pact with Germany on June 18?

A. *Turkey, which the Allies had hoped to keep in their camp.*

Q. On what country did Germany, Italy, and Romania declare war on June 22, followed by Finland and Hungary within the week?

A. *The Soviet Union. Hitler's long-planned Operation Barbarossa was put into effect the same day, as German forces invaded Soviet territory along a 1,000-mile front.*

Q. Did the third member of the Tripartite Pact, Japan, also declare war on the Soviet Union?

A. *No. Japan and the Soviet Union stuck to their own agreed-upon armistice. Neither country wanted a war on two fronts.*

Q. As early as mid-March, Hitler had made a decision as to what group would be given administrative power over con- quered Soviet territory. What was that group?

A. *The SS. This decision led to a long string of atrocities in the course of the war.*

Q. Hitler's machinations once again were turning allies into enemies and vice versa. How long did it take Britain to sign a treaty with the Soviet Union?

A. *Just over three weeks. The pact was signed on July 14; it included a promise of British aid to the Soviet Union.*

Q. The front pages of American newspapers were plastered with bad news from Europe, yet by late June millions of Americans were nevertheless turning to the sports pages first. Why?

A. *"Joltin' Joe" DiMaggio of the New York Yankees was in the midst of his epic hitting streak, which had begun on May 15 and would last until July 17, a total of fifty-six straight games that left all previous records in the dust.*

Q. In July, the British were to bomb more targets in Germany, as well as French ports occupied by German warships, than at any previous time. How successful were these sorties?

A. *The success rate, in terms of hitting selected targets, was very low. Not until the middle of the following year would improved technology allow real precision bombing.*

Q. The German invasion of the Soviet Union was moving very rapidly due to a lack of Soviet preparedness—suspicious as

Stalin had been of Hitler, he had not expected an attack so soon. What was the first major Soviet city that the Germans reached?

A. *German tanks reached the outskirts of Kiev on the eleventh of July.*

Q. Although it was still five months before America would be in the war, what island were U.S. Marines sent to protect in July so that British troops could be withdrawn for duty elsewhere?

A. *Iceland. Its location was so strategic in terms of the flow of Atlantic shipping that once again American isolationists could only mutter about this new step toward involvement.*

Q. In a speech in Des Moines, whom did Charles Lindbergh strike out at as being agitators for war?

A. *American Jews, in a statement that gravely damaged the isolationist movement.*

Q. On July 24, Japan occupied French Indochina. What was the American and British reaction to this event?

A. *Both countries froze all Japanese assets two days later. The United States followed up on August 1 by banning the sale of American oil to any countries other than Great Britain, countries within the British Empire, and countries in the Western Hemisphere. Although Japan was not mentioned by name, this action was meant as a very strong warning to the Japanese, who produced no oil of their own, but instead of causing Japan to back off it pushed them further toward war.*

Q. Given the events in Europe, Roosevelt had asked Congress to extend the draft from one year to thirty months. By how large a margin did the measure pass the House of Representatives?

A. *By one vote.*

Q. Meeting off Newfoundland from August 9 to 12, Roosevelt and Churchill came to the understanding that the United States would do what if the Japanese attacked British or Dutch holdings in the South Pacific?

A. *Without making a formal agreement, it was understood that the United States would then enter the war. They also drew up a statement of democratic principles, derived in part from Roosevelt's State of the Union Message that year, which would be endorsed by fifteen other countries in September. However, this Atlantic Charter, as it came to be known, was never issued except as a communiqué.*

Q. In the summer of 1941, "V" for Victory could be found chalked on walls by resistance fighters all over Europe. This was partially because the word for victory began with a "V" in so many languages. But there was another reason. The Morse code for victory bore a marked resemblance to the first notes of a famous symphony. What was it?

A. *Beethoven's Third, the "Eroica."*

Q. In mid-August, RAF pilots flew thirty-nine Hurricane fighters to what Allied country?

A. *The Soviet Union. The pilots remained until winter, training Soviet pilots to fly the planes.*

Q. Also in mid-August, five thousand exhausted Australian troops at Tobruk were replaced by Free troops from what country under Nazi control?

A. *Free Polish troops came in as replacements.*

Q. British and Soviet troops were sent to another oil-producing country in late August. Name it.

A. *Iran.*

Q. The Germans had made remarkably fast progress into the Soviet Union initially. What, according to the diary of the German Army Chief of Staff Franz Halder, were the Germans beginning to realize in August?

A. *That Soviet forces were much greater than had been thought. The Soviet weaknesses in the war with Finland were proving misleading.*

Q. By September 8, the German army had completely encircled Leningrad on the land side of the city. But the city was protected at the rear by the vast waters of Lake Ladoga. Were there any defenses the Russians had been able to construct on the land side?

A. *Yes. Working feverishly, more than 300,000 members of the Young Communists League and 200,000 Leningrad civilians had surrounded the city with rings of earthworks, antitank ditches, barbed wire, and pillboxes. The earthworks alone added up to more than 600 miles of concentric rings.*

Q. Before the Germans arrived, the most important contents of Leningrad's most famous building were packed and shipped to Siberia. What was the building called and what were its contents?

A. *The Hermitage, Russia's greatest museum, was stripped of its most important old master paintings, sculpture, tapestries, and jewelry; they were crated up in an astonishing four days of round-the-clock work.*

Q. Over the 900 days that the city was besieged, what was the greatest problem for the citizens of Leningrad?

A. *Food. Malnutrition and eventually outright starvation would cause more than a million deaths. If it had not been for Lake Lagoda, over which supplies could be shipped by boat for six months of the year, and by truck when the ice froze to a depth of six feet, the situation would have been even worse.*

Q. On the twenty-sixth of September, one of Russia's most ancient cities fell to the Germans. Name it.

A. *Kiev. German casualties numbered 100,000, Russian 500,000 with another 665,000 Russians captured, according to German figures.*

Q. What order was given by Hitler concerning Polish Jews on October 15?

A. *All Jews found outside the ghettos would be executed on the spot.*

Q. Moving along the same route that Napoleon had taken, with disastrous results, the Germans had moved to within seventy miles of Moscow in the third week of October. They then encountered a natural condition that had also plagued Napoleon. What was it?

A. *Mud. With the autumn rains, the roads became almost impassable.*

Q. On October 17, a new prime minister of Japan was elected. What was his name?

A. *Hideki Tojo, a career army officer from a family of ten. Although he came to be almost as hated as Hitler in America, he was not a dictator.*

Q. After a month-long debate, what laws did the U.S. Congress finally agree to repeal?

A. *The various laws subsumed under the Neutrality Act. Now Roosevelt had a much freer hand.*

Q. By the end of October, the Germans had moved through the endless mud to within thirty miles of Moscow. But now the rain and mud were replaced by snow and the first cases of frostbite began to hit the German soldiers. Why weren't they better equipped for cold weather?

A. *Because Hitler and the army brass had vowed that Moscow would fall before winter. To issue winter clothes, they felt, would undermine the soldiers' confidence that the task could be completed.*

Q. Russian soldiers were used to winter and properly outfitted. What did the United States ship 13 million pairs of to Russia in the course of the war?

A. *Felt boots, which had long been known to be the best defense against frostbite of the feet.*

Q. As in Leningrad, the citizens of Moscow joined in preparing a defense, particularly antitank ditches. How many of those digging these ditches were women?

A. *Seventy-five percent of them were women; in Leningrad half had been women.*

Q. On December 4, the temperature around Moscow fell to 31 degrees below zero. How close were German forces to the city?

   a. 5 miles
   b. 10 miles
   c. 18 miles

A. *The answer is c. That was as close as they would get. On December 6 100 Russian divisions, specially trained for winter fighting, launched a counterattack under General Georgi K. Zhukov. Stalin had fired Zhukov as Army Chief of Staff after the German invasion in a disagreement over strategy, but Zhukov had redeemed himself in Stalin's eyes by his marshaling of the defense of Leningrad.*

Q. In mid-November Japanese Ambassador Nomura had arrived in Washington to negotiate with U.S. Secretary of State Cordell Hull on the terms of a peace treaty between the two nations. What was the main stumbling block from the Japanese point of view?

A. *The absolute insistence by the United States that Japan withdraw all of its troops from China. Japan had invested far too much in its campaigns in China to agree.*

Q. As the negotiations became virtually stalemated, it was clear to Roosevelt as early as November 24 that war with Japan was almost inevitable, and might come with Japanese attacks in the Pacific as early as the twenty-ninth. Where did U.S. military intelligence expect such an attack might be made?

    a. Malaya
    b. Siam
    c. The Philippines

A. *All three were considered likely targets, but Malaya and Siam (Thailand) were regarded as the most likely targets. There was no inkling of the actual scope of Japanese war plans.*

Q. The United States knew that the Japanese consul in Honolulu had been ordered to make reports to Tokyo twice a week on ship operations at Pearl Harbor. Is this true or false?

A. *This is true. Because of its ability to crack most Japanese codes, the United States had a number of clues about the possibility of an attack on Pearl Harbor, but the pieces were never put together and many were ignored. This particular piece of information about the consul's special reports was never even passed on to the military authorities at Pearl Harbor.*

Q. Japan's Pearl Harbor Strike Force set sail from Tankan Bay on November 26. The force consisted of six aircraft carriers flanked by battleships and cruisers. Was this force ever spotted by the United States before the attack on Pearl Harbor?

A. *No. It took a misleading route across the Pacific and was often obscured by bad weather. Another force was spotted in the South China Sea, where its appearance puzzled military intelligence.*

Q. What did the U.S. carrier *Lexington* do on December 5?

A. *It set sail from Pearl Harbor to ferry aircraft to the Marine base at Midway. The carrier* Enterprise *was already at sea on a similar mission to Wake Island. The absence of these ships from Pearl Harbor was one of the few pieces of good luck the United States had.*

Q. On an early December Sunday, Washington, D.C.'s Griffith Stadium was filled with more than 27,000 people watching the Redskins play their final football game of the season against the Philadelphia Eagles. As the game progressed, various politicians and military officers were paged over the public-address system. Why?

A. *The attack on Pearl Harbor was under way. It was December 7.*

Q. Also at the game was a young naval ensign whose war experiences in the Pacific would be recounted in a book and a movie starring Cliff Robertson two decades later. Who was he?

A. *John Fitzgerald Kennedy.*

Q. Edward Tammi, then the assistant director of the FBI, was put on a special telephone hookup in Washington that connected him with J. Edgar Hoover in New York and the chief agent in Honolulu. What did the Honolulu agent do with his telephone?

1941: World War

A. *He held it up to an open window of his office so that Hoover and Tammi could hear the bombs exploding at Pearl Harbor.*

Q. The Japanese airmen attacking Pearl Harbor had photographic blowups showing the location of many of the ships in the harbor. What had these blowups been created from?

A. *Tourist postcards that had been bought in Hawaii.*

Q. A crucial Japanese message indicating extreme interest in ship maneuvers at Pearl Harbor was intercepted by the United States on the morning of December 7. It was spotted by a young woman translator in the code office. She thought it looked very important and took it to superiors. What did they do with it?

A. *Put off decoding it until the next day. They were swamped with work decoding the Japanese diplomatic messages to Ambassador Nomura. This work did make it possible for Roosevelt and Cordell Hull to know that Nomura would be breaking off negotiations when he met with Hull at a 1:00 P.M. meeting the Japanese had urgently requested.*

Q. The request that the meeting with Hull be at 1:00 P.M. had caused some suspicions that Pearl Harbor might be attacked. Why was the time significant?

A. *It coincided with dawn at Pearl Harbor. Army Chief of Staff General George C. Marshall dispatched an immediate warning to Pearl Harbor.*

Q. How long did it take for Marshall's warning to arrive at Pearl Harbor?

A. *More than six hours, arriving long after the attack was over. There was so much static on the army cable line that the message, not even marked "Priority," was sent by Western Union.*

Q. As the first Japanese planes from their carriers flew off to Pearl Harbor, the message, "Tora, Tora, Tora" was radioed to Admiral Nagumo. What do these words mean?

A. *"Tiger, Tiger, Tiger." This was the code to let the admiral know that the attack was a complete surprise.*

Q. Delays in translating the final message from Tokyo at the embassy in Washington, caused Ambassador Nomura to be late for his meeting with Secretary Hull. Did Hull know what was happening at Pearl Harbor?

A. *Yes. He dismissed the ambassador and the envoy who accompanied him with cold anger, but did not reveal that he knew of the attack. In fact, Ambassador Nomura himself did not know.*

Q. Why was a radar sighting of the Japanese planes approaching Pearl Harbor dismissed as nothing to worry about by the duty officer?

A. *He assumed that it was a flight of B-17s that were expected to arrive from California.*

Q. In what configuration were the American planes on the ground at Pearl Harbor when the attack began?

A. *They were parked wingtip to wingtip—sitting ducks.*

1941: World War

Q. The most terrible loss of life at Pearl Harbor was among the crew of the *Arizona,* which was blown out of the water, losing more than 80 percent of its crew of 1,500. Why did the bomb that hit it have such an enormous effect?

A. *It went straight down the smokestack into the engines.*

Q. The battleship *Oklahoma* was capsized by the bombing and rested upside down underwater. More than 400 men were trapped in an intact area of the hull. How long did it take to get them out?

A. *It took divers two days. Only 30 men were ultimately saved from the 400. The battleship* Maryland *nearly capsized but heroic efforts to let in water on the intact side stabilized it.*

Q. Three American planes flying in from the carrier *Enterprise* were shot down by "friendly fire" from the ground. Is this true or false?

A. *True. The situation on the ground was one of total chaos.*

Q. Doris Miller was awarded the Navy Cross for his heroism aboard the battleship *West Virginia* during the Japanese attack on Pearl Harbor. What was unusual about Miller aside from his feminine-sounding name?

A. *Miller was a black man who served as a steward (a cook) aboard the battleship. Although he had never used a machine gun before, he took one over from fallen gunners and shot down at least two and perhaps four Japanese planes. Promoted to petty officer but still a steward, he went down with the* Lipscombe Bay *in November of 1943, but his her-*

oism at Pearl Harbor was a factor in the navy's eventual decision to accept blacks as combat personnel.

Q. The losses at Pearl Harbor were great. Five battleships were either sunk or beached, three others damaged, and ten smaller ships of various classes were destroyed. Of the planes on the ground, 188 were blown apart or consumed by fire. Of the 2,400 military men killed, half came from the *Arizona.* Yet it could have been much worse. Why, for example, did the Japanese fail to blow up the oil depot?

A. *The Japanese planes made two strikes on Pearl Harbor. But the cautious Admiral Nagumo called off a third strike urged by his staff for fear of retaliations against the Japanese carriers. Some historians feel this caution prevented the Japanese from taking total control of the Pacific.*

Q. Which of the following did the Japanese also attack on December 7?

    a.   Singapore
    b.   The Philippines
    c.   Hong Kong

A. *Troops attacked all three from the sea; Guam, Wake Island, and Midway all suffered from air raids. The Japanese had 169 ships and 2,000 aircraft spread out across the Pacific to make coordinated attacks.*

Q. As night approached on the West Coast, what happened in Los Angeles and San Francisco?

A. *The cities were blacked out. An attack on the mainland was deeply feared.*

Q. "Being saturated and satiated with emotion and sensation, I went to bed and slept the sleep of the saved and the thankful." Who is describing his reaction to the attack on Pearl Harbor?

A. *Winston Churchill. The day's events meant that America would be in the war, and he was convinced that with U.S. involvement Hitler and Japan could both be defeated.*

Q. On December 8, 1941, the day after Pearl Harbor, President Roosevelt was to address the full Congress to ask for a declaration of war. The White House head of security felt it necessary to have an armored car to drive Roosevelt to and from Capitol Hill. But by law, no more than $700 could be spent on a government car, and an armored car would have cost much more than that. It turned out, however, that the Treasury Department had an armored car it had seized in a tax case. To whom had the car belonged?

A. *Chicago gangster Al Capone. The car was used until a new one was donated by the Ford Motor Company.*

Q. In his "day that will live in infamy" speech to Congress, did Roosevelt ask for a declaration of war against Germany as well as Japan?

A. *No. He wanted as close to a unanimous vote as possible and felt that if he included Germany there would be some resistance. He had no doubt that a declaration of war against Germany would come soon enough.*

Q. How many members of Congress voted against the declaration of war?

A. *One, Jeannette Rankin, the pacifist representative from Montana, who had also voted against entry into World War I.*

Q. On December 10, the British battleships *Repulse* and *Prince of Wales* were sunk by Japanese bombers east of Malaya. But the British did have some good news in North Africa. What was it?

A. *Rommel finally called off his attempt to take Tobruk (at least for the time being).*

Q. What did Germany and Italy do on December 11?

A. *Declared war on the United States. Roosevelt had been correct in feeling that Hitler could not resist doing so. Congress reciprocated the declaration at once.*

Q. The Japanese continued making strong offensive moves in all areas, and also invaded Borneo. Did the American and British forces have any successes?

A. *No. American forces under General Douglas MacArthur were retreating in the Philippines, British forces were doing the same in Malaya, Wake Island fell on the twenty-first, and Hong Kong on the twenty-fifth.*

Q. Congress amended the Selective Service Act on the nineteenth. All men eighteen to how old were now required to register for the draft?

A. *Up to sixty-five years of age. Those eighteen to forty-four became subject to military service.*

Q. Also on the nineteenth, a series of skirmishes between the British and Italian navies in the Mediterranean came to a disastrous end when the British battleships *Queen Elizabeth* and *Valiant* were sunk in the harbor at Alexandria in Egypt. How were they sunk?

A. *Italian midget submarines placed depth charges under them.*

Q. On the twenty-second Winston Churchill arrived in Washington. He was put up at the White House where the staff was somewhat bemused at one aspect of his daily breakfast. What was it?

A. *Scotch. Otherwise, he drank brandy.*

Q. "Let the children have their night of fun and laughter, let the gifts of Father Christmas delight their play. Let us grown-ups share to the full in their unstinted pleasures before we turn again to the stern tasks and formidable years that lie before us, resolved that by our sacrifice and daring these same children shall not be robbed of their inheritance or denied the right to live in a free and decent world."
Who spoke these words on Christmas Eve, 1941?

A. *Churchill, in a radio address to the American people.*

Q. Churchill and Roosevelt, together with their staffs, worked long hours planning war strategy, and after dinner on the twenty-seventh, Mrs. Roosevelt suggested they take a break. They decided to watch a movie starring Humphrey Bogart. What was it?

A. The Maltese Falcon.

Q. Roosevelt and Churchill gave considerable thought to the forming of a new multinational organization. They had agreed to call it The Associated Powers. But on New Year's Eve, after both men had retired, Roosevelt had a better idea. Early the next morning, with Roosevelt still in his pajamas, he had his chief aide and old friend Harry Hopkins wheel him to Churchill's bedroom. Churchill was delighted with Roosevelt's suggestion that the organization be called the United Nations, pointing out the phrase came from Lord Byron's poem *Childe Harold*. But there was something odd about the situation as the two leaders of the free world agreed upon this important detail. What was it?

A. *Churchill had just had his bath and was stark naked—and utterly unembarrassed. And so began the first year of a truly worldwide war.*

Part Four
1942: America Mobilizes

Q. The Declaration of the United Nations was signed by Churchill, Roosevelt, and the ambassador and foreign minister of two other countries on January 1. What were the two other countries?

A. *The Soviet Union and China. Another twenty-two countries signed the following day. All pledged to resist the Axis nations and not to make any separate peace.*

Q. When the Japanese struck at Pearl Harbor, there were a total of 2.1 million men in the U.S. armed forces. But now a massive buildup was under way. What was the minimum height for a draftee?

a. 5 feet
b. 5 feet 2 inches
c. 5 feet 4 inches

A. *The answer is a. The minimum weight requirement was only 105 pounds.*

Q. If a draftee had vision problems that could be corrected by glasses and at least half his teeth, he was taken. What were the two most common physical attributes or problems that led to rejection?

A. *Flat feet and venereal disease.*

Q. Who was named Commander in Chief of Allied Forces in China on January 3, 1942?

A. *Chiang Kai-shek. At the same time, General Wavell was again given an important active military command as head of a newly formed American-British-Dutch-Australian force known as ABDA, which was charged with holding back the Japanese along a line from Malaya through the Dutch East Indies to Borneo.*

Q. As though thumbing their noses at ABDA, the Japanese invaded what new area on January 11?

A. *The Dutch East Indies.*

Q. Stalin and General Zhukov were once again at odds in early January. One argued that Soviet forces should counterattack the Germans across the entire front. The other felt that despite short-term gains, such a strategy would not leave enough reserves in the long run. Which man took which position?

A. *Stalin wanted to strike across the board and prevailed in the argument, but Zhukov, as usual, turned out to be right.*

Q. In a similarly dictatorial fashion, Hitler had been busy since December doing what to any officer on the Russian front who suggested falling back temporarily, to regroup until spring?

A. *Relieving him of his command. By mid-January all three top generals had been replaced as well as nearly forty other high-ranking officers.*

Q. Where did German submarines begin operating for the first time in mid-January?

A. *Along the East Coast of the United States. There were initially only eleven U-boats involved, but their number soon increased into the twenties.*

Q. On the West Coast, in Hollywood, the words LOCKHEED THATAWAY were painted on the roof of what?

A. *They were painted in huge letters on the roof of a Warner Bros. sound stage. A Lockheed aircraft plant was just down the road. These directions to potential Japanese bomber pilots were regarded as a joke by some, but others suggested that they were merely another reflection of Jack Warner's sense of his own importance.*

Q. At a meeting in Berlin on January 20, Hitler agreed to a new program and Adolf Eichmann was given a promotion. What was discussed at the meeting?

A. *The "Final Solution"—the extermination of the Jews. Eichmann was put in charge of the operation. This meeting later came to be known as the Wannsee Conference.*

Q. Why did General Rommel decide on a counteroffensive against the Allies in Libya on January 21?

A. *He had learned that two Australian divisions were to be withdrawn from North Africa to join the fight against the Japanese in the Pacific. In a surprise attack on the twenty-fifth, Rommel's forces virtually obliterated the British 2nd Armored Division, and four days later Benghazi was retaken by the Germans. The fox was on the prowl again.*

Q. Admiral Kimmel and General Short, who had been in command at Pearl Harbor, were found guilty of what by a Board of Inquiry on the twenty-sixth of January?

A. *Dereliction of duty. Admiral Kimmel had already been replaced as Commander of the Pacific Fleet by Admiral Nimitz in mid-December.*

Q. After Pearl Harbor, Roosevelt and Wendell Willkie had patched up their differences, their election contest forgotten. Willkie was once again supporting Roosevelt on many issues, but there was one problem he couldn't get Roosevelt to listen to him about. He felt strongly that despite improvements, the production of military equipment was still inefficient and disorganized and that a new government office needed to be created to take charge of the matter. He came into the Oval Office one January day to press the idea again, only to find it had already been agreed to. A previous visitor that day had come in and laid down the law on the subject to the president. Who had changed Roosevelt's mind?

A. *Harry Truman had once again made a strong impression on Roosevelt. Thus the very powerful War Production Board was created, with Donald M. Nelson, who had been running the Supplies, Priorities and Allocations Board, as its director. The new position would carry such sweeping powers as to make Nelson, after Roosevelt, the second most powerful man in the country in terms of the economy.*

Q. In Malaya, the situation was worsening for Australian and British troops trying to hold the line against the Japanese. Where did General Wavell give permission for them to retreat to at the end of January?

A. *Singapore, which was none too secure itself.*

1942: America Mobilizes

Q. During January, what had been washing up on the beaches of South Florida that the American public was not told about?

A. *The bodies of sailors from merchant ships sunk by German U-boats. German submarines sank ships with a total tonnage of more than 150 tons during the month. Unused to submarine warfare, many ships failed to take proper precautions in terms of blackouts and radio silence.*

Q. Why were the British angry with the U.S. Navy about the U-boat situation along the East Coast?

A. *Some British ships had been among the victims and the U.S. Navy refused to listen to the very experienced British on how to handle the situation.*

Q. On January 29, the British and the Soviets signed an alliance with Iran. Quite aside from Iran's oil reserves, why would this treaty prove important in the course of the war?

A. *It provided a route by which Allied supplies could be sent to Russia in support of its battle with Germany.*

Q. On February 1, the last automobile assembly line ceased making cars and turned to war production. How many new cars were in stock across the country?

    a.   300,000
    b.   500,000
    c.   725,000

A. *There were 500,000 remaining, which the government doled out on a priority-only basis for the rest of the war.*

Q. Rubber was rationed, in part because the majority of the world's rubber-producing areas were in Japanese hands. But synthetic rubber had been introduced and was widely used for military vehicles. What was the real reason why the government made it next to impossible to buy new automobile tires?

A. *To back up the rationing of gasoline. If your tires were going, you were more likely to stay home. In addition, synthetic rubber was made from petroleum products.*

Q. How much gasoline was allowed per week for a family car?

A. *Beginning in the fall of 1942, only three gallons a week.*

Q. In mid-February the British decided upon a change in strategy for their bombing runs on Germany. Instead of trying to hit factories, they decided to go after what?

A. *The homes of the factory workers, particularly in towns with old wooden homes that would burn easily. By knocking out the work force, it would be possible to greatly slow down production, and the broader target area was much easier to hit.*

Q. Singapore fell to the Japanese on February 15. The Japanese lost 10,000 troops in the effort. What were the British losses?

a. 97,000
b. 138,000
c. 161,000

A. *The loss of 138,000 men made it the single largest military catastrophe in British history. General A. E. Perceval was captured.*

Q. On the nineteenth of February, Japan attacked what country for the first time?

A. *Australia, with a carrier-based air attack on Darwin.*

Q. On February 19 Roosevelt signed an executive order that in retrospect was the most controversial of his decisions during the course of the war. What was the order?

A. *The language of the order was broad but its effect was that 112,000 Japanese Americans were rounded up and sent to internment camps. Two thirds of them were naturalized or native-born Americans.*

Q. Of the following list of men, two were against the internment policy. Which men were they?

    a. Earl Warren, governor of California
    b. Walter Lippman, leading newspaper columnist
    c. Milton Eisenhower, educator and brother of Ike
    d. Attorney General Francis Biddle
    e. J. Edgar Hoover, director of the FBI
    f. Hugo Black, Supreme Court justice

A. *Attorney General Francis Biddle and J. Edgar Hoover! Earl Warren later said that his urging of the internment was the one thing in his career he was ashamed of.*

Q. Were the sons of interned Japanese Americans subject to the draft?

A. *Yes. Eight thousand served in the armed forces, many of them volunteers.*

Q. More than 10 million men were drafted in the course of the war. How many of these declared themselves conscientious objectors and refused to serve?

   a. 25,000
   b. 43,000
   c. 51,000

A. *Just under 43,000, but only the 6,000 men who refused to serve in any capacity were sent to prison. Of the rest, two thirds served as medics or in other noncombatant jobs at the front, and one third worked in camps in the United States.*

Q. How did U.S. soldiers come to be called GIs?

A. *Because everything they wore, fought with, ate, and slept on was marked GOVERNMENT ISSUE.*

Q. GIs stationed where were issued extra shoes, snowshoes, and skis?

A. *Iceland.*

Q. What fast-rising American general became chief of the War Planning Division of the Army General Staff on February 19?

A. *Dwight David Eisenhower.*

Q. On February 23, the first direct attack on the U.S. mainland was made. What country made it and where did it occur?

A. *A Japanese submarine shelled an oil refinery in Santa Barbara, California, but did little damage despite firing twenty-five shells.*

1942: America Mobilizes

Q. What island that had been seized by the Japanese from the United States was bombed by Admiral Halsey's *Enterprise* task force on February 24?

A. *Wake Island. This provided one small piece of good news in a dismal period in the Pacific.*

Q. What was the Avro Lancaster and why was it so important to the British?

A. *The Lancaster was a new class of bombers that went into service during March of 1942. The workhorse of the British air force for the rest of the war, it could carry 22,000 pounds of bombs. Lancasters flew a total of 156,000 sorties and dropped 608,000 tons of bombs over the next three years.*

Q. In March the War Production Board issued orders about the manufacturing of American men's suits. Which of the following were no longer allowed because of the need to conserve cloth?

    a.   An extra pair of trousers
    b.   A vest
    c.   Patch pockets
    d.   Cuffs

A. *All four were disallowed.*

Q. How was the most famous landmark on Beacon Hill in Boston altered in March?

A. *The gold leaf of the State Capitol dome was painted black so as not to serve as a beacon to possible German planes.*

Q. An international naval force, led by the Dutch Admiral Karel Doorman aboard the cruiser *Java*, was routed while trying to prevent a Japanese strike force from landing on the island of Java. What was the last order of Admiral Doorman as his ship sank?

A. *He radioed the two remaining ships in his force to withdraw without trying to search for survivors, and then went down with his ship. Java was taken by the Japanese just over a week later, on March 9.*

Q. Why did General Douglas MacArthur leave the Philippines for Australia on March 12?

A. *He was ordered to Australia by Roosevelt, to take command of all Allied forces in the Southwest Pacific. Upon departing the Philippines, he made his famous statement, "I shall return." In fact, there were many people, especially in the military, who felt he had bungled the defense of the Philippines. He was, however, to prove a great offensive general in the following years.*

Q. The Bataan Peninsula surrounding Manila Bay was dominated by two large mountains and should have been easy to defend. But the American and Filipino forces that had retreated there neglected to extend their line of defense into the jungle, and were outflanked by the Japanese. They established a firm position after falling back again. But their position had now become essentially untenable. Why?

A. *There were 83,000 soldiers and 26,000 civilians cornered in a ten-square-mile area with little food.*

Q. What capital city in Southeast Asia fell to the Japanese in the second week of March?

1942: America Mobilizes

A. *Rangoon, Burma, the port city which the British had made the capital instead of the ancient inland city of Mandalay. With the loss of Rangoon, all supplies for the Allied forces now had to come overland from India. Since the Japanese also controlled the coast of China, it meant that the inland areas of China under Nationalist Chinese sway would now have to be supplied from India.*

Q. What was "the Hump"?

A. *This was the nickname given by pilots to the awesome 500-mile flight over the 15,000 foot Santsung Range that lay between northern India and the Nationalist Chinese stronghold at Kunming. This was the route by which the Chinese were supplied during the rest of the war. A total of 650,000 tons of cargo were flown over this treacherous territory, plagued by monsoon rains for six months of the year and wild gusts of wind that could exceed 200 miles per hour.*

Q. When Major General Edward P. King surrendered to the Japanese at Lawao on the Bataan Peninsula on April 9, it marked the greatest defeat the United States had ever suffered. Was General King's surrender cleared with higher command?

A. *No. On the previous night General Wainwright on Corregidor had insisted that King hold on. But King was certain that would only cost thousands of additional lives in a hopeless cause.*

Q. How many American and Filipino troops had the Japanese expected to capture when surrender came?

    a. 25,000
    b. 50,000
    c. 75,000

A. *They expected the force under King to amount to only about 25,000 men, but it was three times that size. Of the 75,000 men, about 12,000 were Americans, the rest Filipinos. The Japanese had also expected that the prisoners would have their own rations, but in fact the men were already on the verge of starvation, suffering from malnutrition and tropical diseases. Thus the four-day, sixty-five-mile trek through the mountain jungles to the prisoner of war camps the Japanese had built became known as the Bataan Death March. Just over 60,000 men survived the march. The Japanese bayoneted hundreds of Filipinos, thousands were left to die along the way, and some men were even buried alive—although barely so.*

Q. What five German facilities became operational in the spring of 1942?

A. *The extermination camps Auschwitz, Chelmno, Treblinka, Sobibor, and Belsen-Bergen. Auschwitz alone was capable of killing 12,000 human beings a day.*

Q. How many of Poland's 3 million Jews would survive the war?

    a.   400,000
    b.   500,000
    c.   600,000

A. *The answer is* a.

Q. The Allied forces in Burma were continually driven back after the fall of Rangoon. What did General William J. Slim, the commander of the British Burma Corps, set on fire at Yenangyaung on April 15 in order to prevent them from falling into the hands of the Japanese?

A. *The vast oil fields that were the most important resource in Burma. He also destroyed the country's largest power station, which was adjacent to the oil fields.*

Q. On April 18, sixteen B-25 bombers, altered to give them extra fuel tanks, took off from the carrier *Hornet* to fly the nearly 700 miles across the sea to bomb Tokyo. Who was the commander of this expedition?

A. *Lieutenant Commander James Doolittle, the most highly regarded pilot in the Army Air Force and a onetime holder of the world speed record.*

Q. Because the *Hornet* had been spotted, the planes took off 100 miles farther away from Tokyo than had been planned. Did they have enough fuel to return to the carrier?

A. *No, but that return had never been planned. They were to fly on to Nationalist-held airports on the mainland of China. The question was whether there would now be enough fuel to do even that. The bombing raid was a success, but there was not enough fuel left and the crews had to either bail out or crash-land. All but eleven men were led to safety behind Nationalist lines.*

Q. What reprisal did the Japanese carry out in China to punish the Nationalist involvement in the Doolittle raid?

A. *Enraged that the "sacred" air space over the Emperor's palace had been violated, the Japanese killed at least 250,000 Chinese peasants over the next few weeks.*

Q. The Doolittle raid did much to cheer up Americans on the home front, even though the damage to Tokyo was not great, except in psychological terms. More important, the raid caused the Japanese Navy to change its plans. Why?

A. *Full of shame that the Doolittle raid had not been stopped, and fearful that they would soon have to deploy more ships to protect Japan, the Imperial Navy decided to move up the planned attack on Midway, which would prove to be a crucial error.*

Q. To the people of what Mediterranean island did King George VI of England award the George Cross for their heroism in mid-April?

A. *The people of Malta, which continued to be bombarded almost daily.*

Q. Bud Abbott and Lou Costello went on a cross-country tour. To the building of what did they donate their salaries?

A. *A bomber.*

Q. In 1942 The Academy of Motion Picture Arts and Sciences gave a special award certificate to an Englishman who had written, produced, co-directed, starred in, and composed the score for a film about the British Navy. Name the recipient and his still classic movie.

A. *Noel Coward, of all people, created one of the greatest of all war movies in the superb* In Which We Serve.

Q. What famous serviceman's rendezvous opened in the basement of the 44th Street Theater in New York in 1942?

1942: America Mobilizes

A. *The Stage Door Canteen, where stars such as Gypsy Rose Lee, Tallulah Bankhead, Ethel Merman, Marlene Dietrich, and Alfred Lunt and Lynn Fontanne showed up to mingle with the GIs.*

Q. What was an "allotment Annie"?

A. *This was the disparaging name for young women who married GIs headed overseas just to get their hands on the $50 a month allowance and $10,000 life-insurance policy that went to all GI wives. Some were discovered to be married to more than one man at a time.*

Q. The Battle of the Coral Sea, which took place off southern New Guinea May 4 to 8, 1942, was the first battle of its kind in world history. What made it so different?

A. *It was the first battle between aircraft carriers: the Japanese carriers* Shoho, Shokaku, *and* Zuikaku, *and the American carriers* Lexington *and* Yorktown. *Both the* Shoho *and the* Lexington *were sunk, the other carriers damaged. It was not a victory for either side, but it showed that Japanese expansion in the South Pacific could be stopped.*

Q. The Battle of the Coral Sea was engaged to prevent the Japanese from taking Port Moresby on New Guinea. What was so important about Port Moresby?

A. *The Allied air base there was taking on critical importance with the loss of the Philippines. Even as the Battle of the Coral Sea was being fought, General Wainwright surrendered his 15,000 American and Filipino troops on Corregidor. The end would come within a week with the surrender of General Short.*

Q. How many men went down with the *Lexington*?

A. *None. The crew managed to abandon ship while it was still afloat. It was finished off by an American destroyer.*

Q. As the Japanese moved through Burma, what did many of the Burmese peasants do to Indian civil servants and Chinese merchants?

A. *Burma was virtually run by the 1 million Indians in the country and its economy was largely controlled by the Chinese merchants. The peasants hated both, and went on a mad rampage against them. Rape, murder, and arson flamed up across the country. Every town within 200 miles of Mandalay was burned to the ground and the old capital itself burned for almost a month after Burmese helped spread fires started by Japanese bombs.*

Q. General Joe Stilwell, who had been appointed Chief of Staff to General Chiang Kai-shek, had planned to put together a 100,000-man army of Chinese to defend Northern Burma, but the Chinese procrastinated and bungled in every direction. On May 5, Stilwell realized that he was cut off by the Japanese and began to round up a motley group consisting of a few American officers and civilians, some Chinese, a small British ambulance unit, 19 Burmese nurses and their mentor, Dr. Gordon Seagrave, an American Baptist medical missionary who had been born in Burma. The group totaled 114. With few supplies, he led them on a five-day trek through the jungle on foot to India, forcing them to keep moving at a grueling twenty-mile-a-day pace. How many survived?

A. *All 114 made it through, thanks to the fifty-nine-year-old general's incredible will and drive.*

Q. On May 16, after a 900-mile retreat, the remnants of General Slim's forces also reached India. Of the 25,000 men who were under his command, how many made it out of Burma?

    a. 12,000
    b. 15,000
    c. 19,000

A. *The answer is a. In fact, this was regarded as an extraordinary feat, in that the British forces came through largely intact. Of the 13,000 who did not get out, the great majority were not casualties but Burmese Army deserters.*

Q. At the end of May, 45,000 people were left homeless in Cologne, Germany, following a British bombing attack. How many planes had the British sent on this mission?

    a. 500
    b. 700
    c. 1,000

A. *The answer is c. Even training planes with instructors and pupils at the controls were used. Astonishingly, only 40 planes were lost.*

Q. On the twenty-seventh of May, Reinhard Heydrich, the originator of the "Final Solution" plans for the extermination of the Jews, now serving as the German protector in Czechoslovakia, was shot in an assassination attempt in Prague. Who was responsible for this attempt?

A. *Czech resistance fighters who had been trained in England and then parachuted back into their country. Heydrich died a week later. The Nazis' revenge was to completely wipe out the village of Lidice.*

Q. In North Africa, Rommel had been put in a very bad position by the British 150th Brigade. What was the problem?

A. *The British had cut off his supply line. On May 31 he succeeded in reopening it, decimating the 150th Brigade in the process.*

Q. At the same time, British intelligence managed to break the code used by the American military attaché in Cairo. Why would they want to do this?

A. *They believed it was unsafe, and wanted to prove it. Once they broke it, the code was changed—and Rommel lost a valuable intelligence edge.*

Q. Admiral Isoroku Yamamoto, who had planned the attack on Pearl Harbor, believed that he could finish off the American presence in the Pacific in June of 1942. His new plan called for an attack on the American-held Midway Island, but using only half his strike force. The other half was to be kept to the north, ready to come in and catch American rescue forces drawn to Midway from Pearl Harbor in a pincer movement. Were U.S. naval forces aware of his plan?

A. *Yes. The United States had broken the operational code used by Yamamoto, and Admiral Nimitz devised a surprise of his own. He brought the carriers* Hornet *and* Enterprise *close enough to Midway so that while the Japanese planes were attacking the island his own pilots could swoop in on the Japanese fleet.*

Q. At first, the American surprise did not go well. Although the Japanese had barely had time to prepare, the U.S. force having finally been sighted by the Japanese, the fast Japanese Zeros were able to bring down many U.S. planes. How many attacks did the Japanese fleet survive without much damage on June 4?

A. *The first eight assaults. But then came the dive bombers from the* Enterprise *and the* Yorktown, *which had subsequently joined the force after being hastily patched up in Pearl Harbor—the Japanese thought they had sunk the* Yorktown *during the Battle of the Coral Sea.*

Q. Three out of four of the Japanese carriers were now in flames. Admiral Nagumo had to abandon his flagship, the *Akagi.* The surviving carrier, the *Hiryu,* launched a counterattack and succeeded in torpedoing the *Yorktown* so badly that it had to be abandoned. But a mixed force of U.S. planes then hit the *Hiryu* and it too had to be abandoned, its crew taken aboard by support ships. What did the captain of the *Hiryu* and Admiral Yamaguichi—who had come aboard from the burning carrier *Soryu*—do?

A. *They stayed aboard the* Hiryu *and Admiral Yamaguichi ordered that his men torpedo and sink it.*

Q. Connect the categories on the left below with the correct casualty figures in the right-hand column.

a.	Japanese planes	1.	150
b.	American planes	2.	307
c.	Japanese men	3.	3,500
d.	American men	4.	5
e.	Japanese ships	5.	322
f.	American ships	6.	2

A. *a, 5; b, 1; c, 3; d, 2; e, 4; f, 6.*

Q. How long had it been since the Japanese had last suffered a naval defeat?

A. *Three and a half centuries. The Battle of Midway, which was supposed to give the Japanese complete naval dominance in the Pacific, had exactly the opposite effect. The Japanese would never again attempt a major naval offensive in the course of the war.*

Q. The Germans began attacking Sevastapol in Russia on the seventh of June. One of their weapons was called "Dora." What was it?

A. *The largest mortar gun used in World War II, with a 32-inch barrel.*

Q. At the end of the second week of June, four men landed on a beach near Amagansett, Long Island, took a train into Manhattan, had a shopping spree on Fifth Avenue, and had a meal at the famous Dinty Moore's restaurant. Who were these men?

A. *They were German saboteurs who had been landed from a submarine. All had lived in the United States, but they were amateurs at espionage, and had managed to get spotted by a Coastguardsman even as they were changing clothes on the beach. They and another group that landed a few days later in Florida were quickly rounded up. Six were tried and electrocuted, while two who had cooperated with the FBI had their sentences commuted by Roosevelt to thirty years in prison and were released after the war.*

Q. In late May of 1942, fresh supplies, men, and tanks had put the Allied forces in North Africa in a better position than

Rommel. Yet by mid-June, the situation had evened out with Rommel clearly gaining the upper hand. What were the two main reasons why Rommel was able to do better at this point?

A. *Rommel had a superior grasp of strategic positioning in terms of desert fighting, and his Afrika Korps was far better at making quick repairs to damaged or malfunctioning tanks.*

Q. On June 21, Rommel finally took the garrison at Tobruk with the help of Italian forces, capturing 30,000 Allied men and large amounts of stores from food to gasoline. What was his reward from Hitler?

A. *He was made a field marshal. Moreover, his victory gave him the clout to persuade Hitler to allow him to move his forces eastward toward Egypt in pursuit of the retreating Allies. This was done over the objections of other German generals who wanted to step up the attack on Malta. This was one case where Hitler gave in to sentiment and the glory of the moment, and it would prove a bad mistake.*

Q. On June 25, General Eisenhower was given command of U.S. land forces in Europe. What other general had wanted this position?

A. *General Marshall, but, as would be demonstrated in his handling of the disagreements on strategy following the victory at Midway, his talents for persuasion and compromise were far too valuable in Washington.*

Q. Sevastapol fell to the Germans on July 4. They took more than 90,000 prisoners, but the loss of manpower for the

Germans was a cause for concern in Berlin. How many casualties did the Germans suffer?

    a. 15,000
    b. 24,000
    c. 29,000

A. *The answer is* b. *Some German generals felt this number was out of proportion to the gain and were concerned about the number of troops being thrown into the Russian maw. But Hitler by now had complete control over military operations—to disagree with him was to lose one's command. Instead of taking heed of the losses at Sevastapol, he changed plans and decided to attack Stalingrad, which would prove a terrible mistake.*

Q. One of the women working at the Bell Aircraft factory in Marietta, Georgia, a certain Mrs. Longstreet, was the eighty-year-old widow of a general. In what war had her husband been a major figure?

A. *Her late husband, General James Longstreet, had been a Confederate general in the Civil War, referred to by Robert E. Lee as "my old war horse." After the war he became a Republican and served as Grant's ambassador to Turkey.*

Q. In July of 1942, the first Women's Army Auxiliary Corps recruits reported for training. Early in 1943 the "Auxiliary" was dropped as they became a part of the regular Army. Name the director of the WAC, who later became the first Secretary of Health, Education and Welfare under President Eisenhower.

A. *Oveta Culp Hobby.*

Q. What did the acronym WAVES stand for?

1942: America Mobilizes

A. *Women Accepted for Voluntary Emergency Service. More than 77,000 women entered this naval reserve unit, but unlike the WACs, very few were ever dispatched overseas.*

Q. Claire Lee Chennault, a retired Air Corps captain, had served as an adviser to Chiang Kai-shek, retraining his air force and putting together a volunteer group of American pilots and some from other countries. Known as the Flying Tigers, they flew P-40 fighters emblazoned with a shark's teeth design. For seven months after Pearl Harbor they caused havoc for the Japanese, and then were brought under U.S. military control, with Chennault recommissioned as a brigadier general. How many Japanese planes had this small group managed to bring down in the seven months since Pearl Harbor?

A. *At least 300, and possibly half again as many more. They lost only four pilots in that period and their exploits were a great tonic to the American people, providing some of the few encouraging headlines in that period.*

Q. When he was recommissioned, General Chennault took on as his chief of staff Merian C. Cooper, who had been one of the few combat pilots in World War I. Between the wars, Cooper had become a major Hollywood producer. On his second feature film, Cooper served as co-writer, co-director, and co-producer with Ernest B. Schoedsack. The movie, an enormous hit, contains what to this day is the most famous single scene involving an airplane that has ever been filmed. Name the movie.

A. King Kong, *in which Kong, perched atop the Empire State Building, pulls a plane out of midair and hurls it to the ground.*

Q. Throughout July Hitler kept rearranging the assignment of German forces in Russia, in particular, assigning the Fourth Panzer Army first to Army Group A and then back to Army Group B. What was wrong with this strategy?

A. *It meant that his best tank group in Russia was shuttling back and forth instead of fighting and never seemed to be where it was most needed. Hitler was once again demonstrating his inability to stick to a given plan.*

Q. The extent of the convoy system along the East Coast was increased beginning in July, and new command structures were put in place for the transatlantic convoy system. Did these changes improve the situation?

A. *Yes. Losses were considerably cut in both areas.*

Q. Throughout the month, the Japanese added forces on New Guinea. What was their ultimate objective?

A. *Having failed to take Port Moresby from the sea during the Battle of the Coral Sea, the Japanese were determined to take it overland by gaining control of the island to the north.*

Q. With the success at Midway, was the U.S. military command able to quickly formulate future strategy for the Pacific?

A. *No. There was a great deal of contentious disagreement between the services and even between different officers of the same service. There was particularly bad feeling between Navy Chief of Staff Admiral King and General MacArthur, who wanted to be given command of the entire Pacific theater. Roosevelt himself felt that the Midway vic-*

tory had been a thin and lucky one and was extremely worried about the situation in Russia. The patience and calm of Army Chief of Staff General George C. Marshall were of great importance in keeping the situation from getting seriously out of control. In the end Pacific strategy was dictated by the Japanese—intercepted code messages revealed that the Japanese were building an airport on Guadalcanal, right across from the port of Tulagi on Florida Island, which they also controlled.

Q. A U.S. Marine amphibious force landed on Guadalcanal August 7, took Tulagi the next day, and with little difficulty captured the airfield the Japanese had been building. The airfield was named after a hero of Midway, Major Lofton R. Henderson. What had Henderson done at Midway?

A. *He had purposely crashed his damaged plane into the deck of a Japanese carrier, causing a great deal of damage.*

Q. On the eleventh of August a large and heavily protected Allied convoy was sighted on its way to Malta. The Germans and Italians had been lax in keeping track of the buildup of Allied ships around Gibraltar, and despite heavy air attacks that sank more than half the freighters in the convoy, five got through, including the freighter *Ohio,* which had to be towed into harbor. Why was the *Ohio* the most crucial ship of all those in the convoy?

A. *It was carrying fuel desperately needed for the defense of Malta. With these new supplies, the forces on Malta were able to further disrupt the supply lines to Rommel in North Africa, putting him in an increasingly vulnerable position.*

Q. General Bernard Law Montgomery took command of the Eighth Army in North Africa on August 13 and immediately began to build up defenses for an expected attack by Rommel. This command was not supposed to have been Montgomery's, having been given to General W.H.E. Gott on August 6. Why did the change have to be made?

A. *Gott had been killed on his flight back to Egypt the day after receiving the new post. Thus the perfect man for the job was given it by default.*

Q. A new U.S. carrier, the *Independence*, and a battleship, the *Iowa*, were launched in August 1942. How many more carriers would the United States produce before the end of the year?

A. *Four more, as well as another battleship. U.S. military production was now in full swing.*

Q. What military vehicle first produced during World War II was given such nicknames as "The Iron Pony," "Leaping Lena," and "Panzer Killer"?

A. *The Jeep, whose speed and maneuverability over almost any terrain made it an invaluable military tool.*

Q. Winston Churchill met with Stalin as well as U.S. and Free French representatives in Moscow on August 12. The real purpose of this meeting was to apologize to Stalin. What for?

A. *The Allied decision that they were not yet prepared to open a second front against Europe. The Allies wanted to help take the pressure off the Soviets on the Eastern Front by invading Europe, but Allied military leaders were convinced it was impossible to do so until a much greater number of amphibious landing craft existed.*

Q. Rouen, in France, was the first target of what kind of air raid?

A. *The first bombing mission over Europe to involve only U.S. planes took place on August 17.*

Q. On the nineteenth Canadian and British forces, together with some Free French and American troops, launched a raid on the French port of Dieppe. Poor planning and insufficient training led to the capture or death of 3,600 men, along with the loss of over a hundred aircraft, a destroyer, and more than 60 tanks and landing craft. Why did this debacle come to be regarded as an important long-term plus for the Allies?

A. *A great deal was learned about the difficulty of such an assault from the sea, and every lesson was put to use in the planning of D-Day nearly two years later. The difficulties at Dieppe gave credence to the Allied reluctance to open a second front that year.*

Q. The Germans had been making strong progress in Russia all summer. Rostov-on-the-Don had fallen to them in late July and the oil fields of the Caucasus on August 9. By the twelfth of September they had closed to within three miles of what city?

A. *Stalingrad. Ten days later they would reach the center of the city—but crucial areas of it were still held by the Russians.*

Q. The Battle of the Solomon Islands was raging intensely. The U.S. forces had been unable to stop the Japanese from landing fresh troops under cover of darkness, and at sea there were problems of another kind. How was the carrier *Wasp* sunk on September 15?

A. *It was torpedoed by a Japanese submarine.*

Q. To what position was General Leslie B. Groves appointed on September 17?

A. *He was put in charge of all atomic research in the United States. A first-rate organizer, he found the scientists he was dealing with a bit much to swallow, telling his military staff that he had never seen such a collection of "crackpots."*

Q. The Japanese kept coming over the mountains on New Guinea, along the Kokoda trail through the jungle, and had gotten as close to Port Moresby as thirty miles. But the Australian Commander in Chief, General Blamey, arrived on the twenty-third with stern orders from MacArthur to drive the Japanese back. The Australians had a special reason for saving Port Moresby. What was it?

A. *It was less than 300 miles off the Australian coast. With the help of fresh American troops a counterattack was launched that caused the Japanese to begin to withdraw back down the Kokoda trail on the twenty-seventh.*

Q. On October 2, the Stabilization of the Cost of Living Act was passed by Congress. What did this give Roosevelt the power to do?

A. *As with the Selective Service and Training Act, the name for this new law only hints at what it was really about: It in fact*

gave Roosevelt extraordinary power to control wages of all
kinds and all agricultural prices.

Q. The battle of Stalingrad raged on through the month of October. The Germans made some small gains, but the Soviets,
despite any real help from central command, would not let
go. Why was the fighting during this period a problem for
the Germans?

A. *They were approaching the point of total exhaustion.*

Q. Which, if any, of the following places was not an area of
conflict in 1942?
   a. The Aleutian Islands
   b. Madagascar
   c. Cape of Good Hope

A. *All three saw conflict. The Japanese seizure of the islands of*
Kiska and Attu in the Aleutians was coordinated with the
attempted takeover of Midway. Despite the propaganda
value of the Japanese toehold on what was regarded as
American soil, the Joint Chiefs of Staff decided not to waste
resources trying to retake them until a year and a half later.
In Madagascar, the British succeeded in seizing the large
island from the Vichy French and installing a Free French
government; the concern here was largely to keep Mada-
gascar out of Japanese hands. Finally, the liner Laconia,
carrying families of servicemen and Italian prisoners, was
sunk by a U-boat off the Cape of Good Hope.

Q. The Battle of Santa Cruz in the Solomon Islands resulted in
the sinking of the U.S. carrier *Hornet*. The carrier *Enter-*
prise was also heavily damaged, and in fact was the only

surviving carrier in the Pacific. Heavy damage to a Japanese carrier aside, it appeared to be a Japanese victory. But the Japanese nevertheless withdrew. Why?

A. *Because they had suffered great losses in planes and pilots, due to the superb efforts of the gunners of the battleship* South Dakota.

Q. The U.S. government began printing three billion of these a month. What were they?

A. *Ration stamps, red ones for meat, fish, and dairy products and blue ones for canned goods. Prices were constantly being adjusted by the Office of Price Administration so that no one could be sure how many ration stamps would be needed for a given item from one week to the next. Nor could anyone guess what there might be a shortage of next. Cigarettes were often in short supply, but everything from tea to hair curlers could suddenly become scarce.*

Q. Name the future president who was for a short time one of the 60,000 full-time workers in the rationing bureaucracy.

A. *Richard Nixon, before accepting a navy commission despite his Quaker religion. The experience, he later said, made him more conservative because he was so appalled by the amount of government red tape involved.*

Q. The ration office in Philadelphia had to close down for a short period because it had neglected to issue itself fuel coupons. True or false?

A. *True. There were thousands of such glitches, stories that made everybody feel better.*

1942: America Mobilizes

Q. Of the five following commodities, which three were most likely to cause a truck carrying them to be hijacked, according to the FBI?

    a. Liquor
    b. Meat
    c. Rayon
    d. Shoes
    e. Cigarettes

A. *The top three were liquor, rayon, and shoes. The last may seem surprising, but only two pairs per year could be bought per person.*

Q. What did millions of women ask a friend to do for them with an eyebrow pencil?

A. *Draw a fake seam down the back of their legs so that it looked as though they were wearing stockings instead of merely leg makeup.*

Q. Within the War Production Board, a special Smaller War Plants Division was created with former Congressman Maury Maverick as its head. Maverick hated bureaucratic jargon and coined a new word for it. What was it?

A. *Gobbledygook.*

Q. What mode of transportation became profitable for the first time since 1927 in 1942?

A. *Rail travel. Because of gasoline rationing, millions of Americans went back to riding trains. Since this was also the primary way of travel for military personnel, the trains were often packed like sardine cans.*

Q. A number of comic book heroes, like Joe Palooka, quickly ended up in uniform once the United States entered the war. But Superman was 4-F—true or false?

A. *True. It was felt that it would be demoralizing to the regular fighting men to have Superman involved in the war.*

Q. There was a new service branch called Women's Air Force Service Pilots (WASP) that eventually had 1,500 members. Why were these women pilots preferred over men for ferrying duty?

A. *Because they often reached their final destinations hours ahead of male pilots, who were prone to pursue women during refueling stops.*

Q. The Battle of El Alamein had been initiated on October 23 with Montgomery's attack on Rommel's position, which was heavily protected by minefields and barbed-wire defenses. At the beginning, Montgomery had 195,000 men to 104,000 on the German side, and 1,000 tanks, twice as many as Rommel. Ironically, about 10 percent of Montgomery's tanks were American; they had been promised to Churchill by Roosevelt the previous June as the two leaders met at Hyde Park—the very day that Rommel captured Tobruk. It took ten days for Montgomery, even with the superior forces he had been building for more than two months, to break through the minefields. But his brilliant strategy kept Rommel off guard and by November 3, against Hitler's orders, he began to withdraw. How many operative tanks did Rommel have left at this point?

A. *Only 20.*

Q. Both Rommel and Montgomery were men of great personality, even eccentricity in purely military terms—Rommel with his goggles taken from a captured British officer early in the North Africa campaign, Montgomery with his famous beret and pullover sweaters—and both made great efforts to get to know their men. Both were enormously respected by their troops (and opposing troops); both had great tactical brilliance. But there was one great difference between them. What was it?

A. *Rommel was always itching to get going, ready or not, and for a master improviser, that often paid off. Montgomery wanted to have everything in place before making a move, but was still capable of improvising if necessary. In the Battle of Alamein, Montgomery's emphasis on preparedness paid off. If Rommel had had the supplies promised him by Hitler—who was obsessed with the campaign in Russia— everything might have been different. For nearly two years, Rommel had been the right man in the right place—now it was Montgomery's turn.*

Q. On November 8, Allied forces under the command of Eisenhower launched Operation Torch against French North Africa. This was a daring plan to capture three widely separated major ports from the sea: Casablanca in Morocco, and Oran and Algiers in Algeria. The operation was blessed with a major piece of luck—or German incompetence. What was it?

A. *Once again German intelligence was caught napping. Although 500 British and American ships were converging for the attack, the Germans didn't wake up to what was happening until a few hours before the attack and then misconstrued the situation, thinking Malta was involved.*

Q. There was some French resistance at Algiers, but it was put down by the invading Allied forces in less than a day. But at

Oran the story was different. Resistance was fierce and took thirteen days to overcome. The memory of what event in June of 1940 spurred the Vichy French in Oran to such strong resistance?

A. *The destruction by British bombers of the French fleet at Mers-el-Kebir following the fall of France.*

Q. The British and Americans had been trying for several days to persuade Admiral Jean-Louis-Xavier-François Darlan, the commander of all Vichy forces—who happened to be in Algiers at that very moment on a private visit—that his cooperation in the long run would be beneficial to France. Although long a bitter enemy of England and the chosen successor to Marshal Pétain as head of the Vichy government, he was extremely torn. What did he finally do?

A. *He ordered a cease-fire in Casablanca just before the invasion was begun. He was immediately repudiated by Pétain, but Hitler was convinced Darlan had not acted alone and the Vichy areas of France were promptly occupied by German and Italian forces. Darlan was assassinated on December 24 in murky circumstances by a student who was supposedly acting on orders of the French Resistance. Despite his having gone over to the Allies, the Resistance did not trust him.*

Q. Once the French North African ports had been taken, the Operation Torch plan called for Allied forces to move overland in a great push to take the ports of Tunis and Bizerte. How successful was this aspect of the plan?

A. *It met with forceful counterattack that would continue for months.*

116

Q. In the midst of the battle that was finally to turn the tide for American forces in the Solomon Islands and assure the complete occupation of Guadalcanal two and a half months later, the U.S. destroyer *Juneau* was sunk on November 14. The loss was given particularly heavy newspaper coverage because of the deaths of five men aboard the ship. Who were they?

A. *The Sullivan brothers of Waterloo, Iowa. They had joined the navy almost immediately after Pearl Harbor, where their great friend William Ball, with whom they had grown up, was killed. They had requested that they all be assigned to the same ship. Their surviving sister joined the WAVES and a new destroyer was named* The Sullivans *in their honor.*

Q. Four freighters, with a thirteen-ship escort, sailed from Gibraltar to Malta at the end of the third week of November. What was remarkable about this particular voyage?

A. *It was almost without incident, with only one escort ship being hit. Although there would be scattered attacks in the future, it was now possible for the heroic people of Malta to come out from the caves they had dug into the sandstone of the island and begin to put their lives back together.*

Q. With winter hard on the land, what did the Soviets undertake on November 19?

A. *They began a massive counterattack against the Germans, with a determination to free Stalingrad and regain the oil fields of the Caucasus. A half million fresh troops were involved, as well as 900 newly developed tanks and an even greater number of attack planes. They quickly surrounded Stalingrad, effectively sealing as many as 250,000 German troops inside.*

Q. Why was the French fleet of more than seventy ships, including three battleships, scuttled at Toulon Harbor on the twenty-seventh?

A. *By agreement with the Vichy government, the Germans had stayed out of Toulon. When they occupied it, Admiral Laborde ordered the immediate destruction of the fleet.*

Q. What happened at a top-secret laboratory at the University of Chicago on December 2, 1942?

A. *The first controlled and sustained atomic chain reaction was created.*

Q. Who said to Lieutenant General Robert L. Eichelberger, on December 5, "I want you to take Buna or not come back alive."

A. *General MacArthur, fed up with the slow progress against the Japanese on New Guinea, gave one of his little motivating talks to the man he had handpicked to get things moving.*

Q. A German force sent to relieve Stalingrad was stalled in the third week of December, and in danger of being encircled by Soviet forces. There was considerable feeling that General Paulus should lead his forces in a fight to break out of the Stalingrad trap. Why did he refuse?

A. *He said he did not have enough fuel to try it, thus ensuring the disaster to come.*

Q. The U.S. soldiers on Guadalcanal were having as difficult a time as ever, gaining ground with agonizing slowness. Yet the battle for the island was almost over. Why?

1942: America Mobilizes

A. *A combination of air strikes and PT-boat maneuvers were making it almost impossible to resupply the Japanese forces on the island, which were in much worse shape physically from lack of food than their tenacious fighting indicated.*

Q. The few people in the American government who were aware of what was going on in terms of atomic research were against sharing information with the British except in cases where British research directly overlapped the American effort. Roosevelt backed up this view at the end of December, much to the dismay of the British. Why was there so much concern in this area?

    a.   There was fear that the British could not keep as tight a security lid on what was happening as was desired

    b.   The Americans wanted to be certain that they developed the atomic bomb before anyone else

    c.   There was a feeling that the British were trying to hook a free ride in terms of developing atomic energy for peacetime uses in a postwar world

A. *All of these played a part but it was, rather oddly, the sense that the British were hooking a free ride that was at the forefront. The fact that this should be the chief concern makes clear that American confidence that Germany and Japan would be defeated was growing steadily as 1942, quite possibly the most terrible year in human history, ground to an end.*

Part Five

1943: A World in the Balance

Q. *The* movie of 1943 was *Casablanca,* set in 1940. But it was not Humphrey Bogart (in a role turned down by Ronald Reagan) and Ingrid Bergman meeting in the real city beginning on January 14. Who did?

A. *Roosevelt and Churchill spent ten days in the fabled port, once again in Allied hands, planning overall strategy.*

Q. The main thing Churchill wanted out of the Casablanca Conference was an agreement that once North Africa had been rid of the Germans and Italians, the next step would be an invasion of Sicily and then Southern Italy. Why did he want this so much?

A. *Churchill came to the conference in a difficult position. He was on public record as favoring an assault on Northern Europe in 1943, and had come close to promising Stalin that an Allied opening of a Second Front would occur. Yet he was convinced that it would not be doable until 1944. He needed a way out, and was convinced that if the United States committed itself to taking Sicily and Southern Italy, that would absorb so many troops and armor that it would inevitably prove necessary to postpone the invasion of Europe. The U.S. military had not thought that far ahead, and to the degree that they had, there was internal dispute. Thus they agreed to the Sicily venture without fully understanding the potential consequences. Churchill felt he was off the hook.*

Q. After the last pockets of Japanese resistance were overcome between Gona and Buna on New Guinea, on January 21, General MacArthur was full of boasts about what had been accomplished. How much credit did he give the Australian troops who had done most of the jungle fighting?

A. *Almost none, hardly ever mentioning them, referring instead to "Allied forces" and most of all to "American troops." The Australians were not pleased and limericks about MacArthur's self-importance began to spread among Australian troops.*

Q. In the battle of Gona and Buna alone, 1,600 Allied soldiers had been killed. This was one of the heaviest casualty lists, in terms of the number of troops involved, during the entire war in the Pacific. A famous photograph was taken of dead Marines lying on the beach at Buna. When was this photograph published?

A. *It did not appear until nearly two years after the war and caused great shock when it appeared in* Life *magazine. In fact, no photograph showing nothing but American dead was ever published in the course of the war; there were photographs that showed fallen Americans, but they were always surrounded by charging comrades who were still very much alive. To MacArthur's credit, once he had recovered from his initial fit of boasting and realized how high the casualties were on New Guinea, he said to his staff, "No more Bunas."*

Q. The British occupied Tripoli, Libya, on January 23. Why was this not the prize it might have been?

1943: A World in the Balance

A. *The Germans were able to take large amounts of stores with them and also blew up numerous installations in the port. It took almost a month to make the port usable again.*

Q. After completing *Gone With the Wind* in 1939, the actor Leslie Howard returned to England, where he produced and starred in a series of patriotic movies including *Pimpernel Smith* and *Spitfire*. In January of 1943, he was sent on a secret mission to the governments of Spain and Portugal to help persuade them to join the Allies or remain neutral. As he was returning to England on January 24, his plane was attacked by Nazi fighters and he was killed in the crash, his death mourned by millions around the world. Whose plane did the Nazis think they were shooting down?

A. *Winston Churchill's. He flew home from Casablanca that same day following his meetings with Roosevelt.*

Q. On the twenty-seventh of January, 55 bombers struck at the German industrial town of Wilhelmshaven. In what way was this a first?

A. *The bombers were American; it was the first time U.S. planes had been dispatched to hit a German target.*

Q. General F. M. von Paulus, who had been in command of the German forces at Stalingrad from the start, was made a field marshall by Hitler on January 30. Why was this extremely ironic?

A. *Surrounded by the Soviet Army, he was forced to surrender the following day. Hitler had refused to allow such a surrender a week earlier, and in fact the real reason he had given the honor to Paulus was that, since no German field*

125

*marshal had ever surrendered, Hitler hoped Paulus would
either continue fighting or commit suicide.*

Q. How many German soldiers had died at Stalingrad in the
previous month?

   a. 40,000
   b. 70,000
   c. 100,000

A. *At least 100,000 were dead, and another 90,000 were taken
prisoner, of which only about 5,000 would ever return to
Germany. Huge losses of equipment and supply planes
would hamper the Germans for the rest of the Russian campaign.*

Q. By the ninth of February, Guadalcanal was at last fully in the
hands of the Americans. Some 10,000 of the surviving Japanese troops had been ferried out by destroyers in the previous few days. What had these ship movements led the
Americans to believe was happening?

A. *They thought the Japanese were bringing in fresh troops,
and were preparing for a major battle.*

Q. Even with this strategic evacuation, 10,000 Japanese were
killed in the course of the battle for Guadalcanal and Tulagi.
Did the United States lose fewer men, more, or about the
same number?

A. *They lost only 1,600, but the tenacity of the Japanese in the
face of such huge losses of their own was an omen of how
difficult a task the Allied forces would have in retaking other
South Pacific islands where the Japanese were more entrenched.*

1943: A World in the Balance

Q. On February 22, the British forces at Thala in Tunisia, which had been involved in fierce fighting with Rommel's panzer troops during the night, were reinforced by an American artillery regiment. How long had it taken the regiment to make the nearly 800-mile trek from the port of Oran?

A. *They did it in only four days and almost certainly saved the day for the British, as Rommel drew back after assessing the imposing American armaments.*

Q. The Japanese sent a convoy of 6,000 men to relieve their forces in northern New Guinea. They had been assured that heavy cloud cover would last for several days, but it began to break up on March 1. The convoy was spotted and 200 Mitchell bombers from the Fifth U.S. Air Force were sent to attack the next day, under clear skies. The bombers devastated the convoy with a new technique called "skip bombing." What did this term mean?

A. *It involved dropping the bombs in such a way that they skipped across the water like a stone across a pond, slamming into ships like torpedoes. Almost two thirds of the Japanese soldiers were killed as their ships went down one after another, and more than sixty Japanese aircraft sent to protect the convoy were also lost. Only four American fighter planes went down in the action.*

Q. Allied bombers began a five-month campaign against what area of Germany on March 5?

A. *The Ruhr Valley, the heart of Germany's industrial strength. A thousand Allied planes would eventually be lost but the disruption of German manufacturing was regarded as essential.*

127

Q. In early April the Japanese put 60,00 prisoners of war to work in Burma building what?

A. *A new rail line. A fictionalized account of this effort was told in the 1957 Oscar-winning best picture,* The Bridge on the River Kwai.

Q. Meeting in Salzburg in the second week of April, Hitler and Mussolini decided that they must continue to fight for the control of North Africa. Given what was occurring in North Africa, how should this decision be characterized?

A. *Any adjective from "foolhardy" to "inexplicable" will do. The Axis forces were on the run from the tank forces of Montgomery and General Patton, who had arrived with Operation Torch. If they had been pulled out at this point they could have been put to far better use elsewhere.*

Q. The Germans made an announcement on April 12 of the discovery of mass graves containing more than 4,000 corpses in the Katyn Forest. Who were these slaughtered men?

A. *Polish officers, whom the Soviets had murdered instead of holding them captive. The Soviet Union denied until 1990 that it had done this.*

Q. Seventeen American pilots took off from Henderson Field on Tulagi in P-38s on April 18, 1943—a year to the day since Doolittle's raid on Tokyo—and arrived over the island of Bougainville precisely as a plane carrying Japanese Admiral Isoruku Yamamoto entered the same air space. Eight of the P-38s went after the six Japanese escort fighters while the others concentrated on bringing down two planes, one carrying Admiral Yamamoto, the other, which had not been expected, carrying Admiral Ugaki. Ugaki survived the crash of his bomber into the sea, but Yamamoto was already dead from a bullet through his head as his bomber crashed into the jungle. Why did the United States keep it a secret that they had shot down Japan's top admiral?

A. *The U.S. military did not want the Japanese to realize that they had cracked another important code, and had known precisely where Yamamoto, a famously punctual man, would be at the moment of the attack. They thus allowed the Japanese to think that Yamamoto's death was simply a piece of very bad luck and that the U.S. planes did not realize what they had accomplished.*

Q. The body of a man in the uniform of a British major, with high-level papers suggesting that the Allies planned to attempt to free Greece, was found off the Spanish coast at the end of April. Who was this man?

A. *"The Man Who Never Was," to use the title of a book published after the war and made into a 1953 movie. The body was of an unknown corpse released into the sea from a British submarine as a red herring to distract the Germans from the planned invasion of Sicily. The carefully prepared fake papers were passed on to the Germans and did their job, backed up by increased resistance efforts in Greece.*

Q. On May 7, American and British forces took Tunis and Bizerte almost simultaneously. What began to happen within the next three days in North Africa?

A. *The remaining German and Italian forces surrendered. Two months earlier Rommel had left Africa to return to Germany. He had met with both Mussolini and Hitler and ad-*

vised them to get out of Africa, but they refused to listen. In the end, a quarter of a million Axis soldiers were captured in May, half of them German. Given the terrible losses the Germans had suffered at Stalingrad, this further debacle would greatly intensify the Nazi's manpower problems.

Q. What did the SS blow up in the Warsaw ghetto in mid-May?

A. *The synagogue. The ghetto lay in ruins, and 14,000 Jews had been killed since the uprising began a month earlier. Another 40,000 had been sent to extermination camps.*

Q. The American Liberator B-23 came into service in May of 1943. It had an eighteen-hour flying time. Why was this particularly important?

A. *It meant that surveillance of U-boats in the Atlantic could be greatly increased—there would no longer be a mid-Atlantic gap. By May 22, U-boat attacks on convoys in the North Atlantic were discontinued because the losses of German submarines had become too high.*

Q. The British General F. E. Morgan was given a newly created command—Chief of Staff to the Supreme Allied Commander—as a result of the nearly two-week conference in Washington between Roosevelt, Churchill, and their military leaders during the middle weeks of May. What was General Morgan to start planning for?

A. *D-Day, which had been given a target date of May 1, 1944.*

Q. Two major factories in Antwerp, Belgium, were bombed in May of 1943. Why were the Germans astonished that they would be attacked?

1943: A World in the Balance

A. *The factories were originally built and operated by Ford and General Motors.*

Q. After the German defeat at Stalingrad, it was clear to the Soviets that the next likely German attack would come in the area around the small city of Kursk in the Ukraine. Who said, "Whenever I think of this attack, my stomach turns over."

A. *Hitler, who had been greatly unnerved by the disaster at Stalingrad. The casualties his forces had suffered in Russia were causing him to lose sleep—especially since his refusal to withdraw at every turn had greatly increased the losses. But it seemed necessary to attack at Kursk, trying to catch the Soviet forces in a pincer movement between the German North Army and the German South Army. Otherwise, the Soviet forces would have an opportunity to build up their strength unmolested.*

Q. As the Battle of Kursk approached, the Red Army forces totaled 6.5 million men, even though at least 3 million Russian soldiers had been captured by the Germans, with uncounted numbers killed. What was the size of the German force in Russia?

    a.   3.1 million
    b.   3.7 million
    c.   4.2 million

A. *The answer is a. Over 2 million of the German forces were poised to strike at Kursk, along with 6,000 tanks and 5,000 aircraft. The Russians had slightly larger forces and armaments and had dug themselves in around Kursk to a formidable extent.*

Q. The Battle of Kursk began on July 5. The attack date had been postponed from May by Hitler. Why?

A. *In part it was because he dreaded it, but it was also to allow for new model Panther tanks to be supplied to the front.*

Q. The Battle of Kursk was the greatest confrontation of tanks in the history of the world. It was to become primarily a tank battle after the first two days, because the aircraft on both sides became irrelevant. Why did this happen?

A. *The battle was engaged at such close quarters that it became almost impossible to strike the enemy without knocking out forces on both sides. In addition, the battle was so fierce that the entire area was clouded over by dense black smoke from burning tanks. By the twelfth of July, it was over, with the Soviets the clear victors despite enormous losses. The German losses were such, in manpower, tanks, and planes, that they would never again be able to mount a major offensive. The Allied air strikes on Germany were by then unremitting, disrupting military production to the point that the Germans would never be able to catch up to the strength they had before Kursk. The Russians, on the other hand, would continually increase their military production. From now on the Germans would be on the defensive, and Kursk would go down as one of history's most significant battles.*

Q. Even as the Battle of Kursk was raging, there was more bad news for the Germans as the Allies launched a July ninth invasion where?

A. *Sicily, which began with paratroop landings which were only partially successful because the forces were dropped over too large an area, a problem that was largely due to inexperience in this kind of invasion. Sea landings began the next morning.*

Q. The Allied diversions that had suggested an invasion of Greece had succeeded in confusing the Germans. Hitler thought Sardinia might be the target instead of Greece. But Mussolini correctly guessed it would be Sicily. Why didn't he ask for German help in defending the large island?

A. *Mussolini found himself increasingly cowed by Hitler; he was simply afraid to ask.*

Q. By the sixteenth, the Allied forces were making sufficient headway in Sicily for Churchill and Roosevelt to issue a joint statement to the Italian people calling for what?

A. *Surrender, with a further suggestion that they overthrow Mussolini. The point was backed up by air raids on Rome.*

Q. From the last week of July into early August, the RAF repeatedly bombed German cities. How many people did they render homeless in this period?

   a. 500,000
   b. 800,000
   c. 1 million

A. *At least 800,000 lost their homes and there were 50,000 deaths as a result of the bombing.*

Q. On July 25, what did the Grand Council of the Fascist Party do?

A. *Arrested Mussolini and replaced him with Marshal Pietro Badoglio.*

Q. Since May, American forces had been involved in trying to drive the Japanese out of the Aleutian Islands. They had

133

retaken Attu and were now concentrating on Kiska. On the second of August they bombarded the island heavily. Why was this ironic?

A. *The Japanese had already left. The same thing had happened on Attu. Indeed, this entire campaign was a waste of resources that could have been put to better use in the South Pacific, but home-front politics had made it necessary to finally dislodge the Japanese from this outpost of "American soil."*

Q. Beginning on August 13, a ten-day British-American meeting took place in Quebec, first between military leaders, with Churchill and Roosevelt joining in later. Churchill's agreement to the appointment of General Dwight Eisenhower as Supreme Commander of the Allied invasion of Europe was counterbalanced by the appointment of Admiral Lord Louis Mountbatten as head of a new Southeast Asia Command to be known as SEAC. But the most far-reaching agreement concerned a secret project. What was it?

A. *The development of the atomic bomb. Despite American military protests, Roosevelt had finally ordered that all information concerning the bomb be shared with the British, and the two countries agreed not to use the bomb against one another, or against another country without prior consultation, and not to give any information to any other country.*

Q. Sicily was entirely in Allied hands by August 17. But the victory was tainted in a way that led to later problems on the Italian mainland. What had happened?

A. *100,000 Axis troops, 40,000 of them German, had been allowed to escape to Italy proper.*

1943: A World in the Balance

Q. Kharkov, the Russian city that was the most fought over in the course of the war, had been retaken from the Germans in February by the Soviets, who then lost it again in mid-March. On the twenty-second of August the Germans began to evacuate it again. Was this approved by Hitler?

A. *Yes. General Eric von Manstein, the commander of the Army Group South, had on several occasions managed to persuade Hitler to withdraw, the only general Hitler was willing to take such advice from. Historians generally regard Manstein as the best of all Hitler's generals, and even Hitler apparently understood that he could not dismiss Manstein or his arguments as he did those of so many other military men.*

Q. What distinguished the two Russian women Lilya Litvak and Katya Budanova?

    a.   They were heroines of the siege of Leningrad
    b.   They were Russian singers beloved of the troops
    c.   They were fighter plane aces

A. *Lieutenant Litvak and Lieutenant Budanova were each responsible for shooting down at least half a dozen German planes as fighter pilots.*

Q. What were "Belle o' the Brawl," "Pistol Packin' Mamma," and "Grin 'n Bare It"?

A. *Names stenciled onto the fuselages of American bombers based in England.*

Q. "Chaff" or "window" (the respective American and British code names) was often dropped by bombers as they were en route to a target. What was it?

A. *These were strips of aluminum foil that played havoc with radar. A drop of 2,000 strips gave the electronic appearance of a B-17.*

Q. Window was used to draw German fighters to Berlin while an Allied force bombed the rocket facilities at Peenemünde on August 18. That attack and one the previous day at two other sites caused the Chief of Staff of the Luftwaffe Hans Jeschonnek to do what?

A. *He committed suicide after being upbraided by Hitler for not having done more to prevent the attacks, even though the Luftwaffe had shot down more than 90 of the 850 RAF bombers involved in the two raids.*

Q. In late August, Allied forces finally captured New Georgia and Arundel. Where were these islands located?

A. *The Solomon Islands. A year and a half after driving the Japanese out of Guadalcanal, the Allies were still trying to secure the rest of the Solomons. Innumerable land and sea battles as well as bombing raids, with great losses on both sides, had still not settled the issue, as the securing of individual islands and even of particular hills seesawed back and forth in actions that came to seem to American troops like a nightmare from which they would never wake. The same was true on New Guinea. The Allies would not finally prevail in either arena until well into 1944.*

Q. What was the new word American GIs gave to the English language to describe military incompetence?

A. *Snafu. This is usually defined as short for "Situation Normal, All Fouled Up," but that is not exactly how they said it.*

1943: A World in the Balance

Q. Name two things recently perfected in U.S. laboratories that were instrumental in saving the lives of American servicemen. One was "defensive" and used in all theaters of war. The other was "offensive" and was particularly important in the South Pacific and other tropical areas.

A. *The "defensive" weapon was penicillin, first created by Dr. Alexander Fleming in 1929 but further developed at the U.S. Department of Agriculture laboratory at Peoria, Illinois. In all previous wars, the majority of deaths had resulted from bacterial infection of wounds. The "offensive" weapon was DDT, which we now know has very serious environmental side effects, but during World War II the spraying of DDT drastically cut down on the incidence of malaria and typhus among servicemen.*

Q. On the home front, the call of Secretary of Agriculture Claude R. Wickard for Americans to plant Victory Gardens had become a whopping success. What percentage of American vegetable production did Victory Gardens account for by the summer of 1943?

A. *Over 20 million Victory Gardens produced one third of all vegetables.*

Q. Although an Italian surrender agreement was signed on September 3 in Sicily, it was not announced until five days later. Why not?

A. *The Allies did not want the Germans to know about the surrender until they could begin to invade the mainland. The first forces, under Montgomery, had landed at dawn that very morning near Reggio at the toe of Italy's boot. The announcement was made the night of September 8 as the British prepared to land at Taranto on the inner heel of*

*the boot and both American and British forces at Salerno,
south of Naples.*

Q. Why did the Italian government leave Rome on September 9?

A. *Despite the delayed surrender announcement, Italian forces
had not been sufficiently well organized to hold the city and
the Germans quickly took it over.*

Q. The forces at Taranto had met with little resistance but did
not have the armored equipment to move forward. What
kind of resistance was encountered at Salerno?

A. *Strong German resistance made it impossible to move beyond the beachhead positions for nearly ten days. A German
counterattack on the thirteenth ripped apart the 2nd Battalion of the 143rd U.S. Infantry. In one of the truly heroic
actions of the war, every U.S. soldier in the vicinity, from
clerk to cook, was given a gun to help protect two American
field-artillery battalions, who managed to fire their guns at
a rate that was as fast as any achieved in the entire war, and
the Germans were driven back.*

Q. On the twelfth, Mussolini was rescued by the Germans in a
harrowing escapade from the Abruzzi mountains where he
was being held and taken to Germany. In a meeting with
Hitler, he was told to return to Italy and form a new Fascist
state in the north of his country. What was there about
Mussolini that might have suggested to Hitler that this was
not a good idea?

A. *Mussolini was losing his mind. In the months to come he
would start comparing himself to Jesus Christ and Napo-*

leon, denigrating the Italian people as a nation of ice-cream eaters, and generally coming apart at the seams.

Q. Why was a mere regiment of German infantrymen able to impede the advance to Naples from Salerno by three British divisions for nearly a week in late September?

A. *The route from Naples to Salerno was—and is—through a series of mountain passes.*

Q. Starting at eight in the morning on September 21, 1943, a beloved American entertainer spoke live on the CBS radio network a total of sixty-five times over a marathon sixteen hours urging Americans to buy war bonds. Who was this entertainer?

A. *Kate Smith, who roused Americans to buy $40 million worth of bonds as a result of this single effort. All over the country juke boxes were playing her recording of a song written by Irving Berlin during World War I but virtually forgotten until she revived it, a song called "God Bless America." Roosevelt once said of the large lady with the huge voice, "Kate Smith is America."*

Q. As a result of the war and the drafting of millions of young men, American colleges and universities had feared that many of them would have to shut their doors, that there would be too few students to make it economically feasible to keep them running. What saved them?

A. *They were used to train officers, technicians, and medical personnel. In the course of the war, the U.S. government paid to have a million and a half men specially trained—and the GI bill after the war proved a bonanza for American educational institutions.*

Q. The citizens of what Italian city tried to overthrow the Germans at the end of September?

A. *Neapolitans had had enough, and began fighting the Germans from street to street. Large numbers of civilians were killed but they kept fighting until the Allies finally marched into the city on October 1.*

Q. Why did the Soviets push so hard to get men and tanks across the Dnieper River in late September and early October?

A. *The west bank of the river would offer a strong line of defense for the retreating Germans, the broadness of the river making it very difficult to cross under fire. The Soviets established a beachhead at Lyutezh on the fifth of October, managing to ferry across sixty tanks. But the Germans held many other strong points along the river.*

Q. What country declared war on Germany on October 13?

A. *Italy—the war-weary Italian people had now come full circle and welcomed Allied forces as they fought their way slowly up the boot on both sides, held back by terrible weather and tenacious German resistance.*

Q. In mid-October a cherished belief of the American military was dealt a severe blow when 291 B-17s ("Flying Fortresses") made a daylight raid on a factory in Schweinfort, Germany, that was a major producer of ball bearings. What happened?

A. *Nearly half the planes were damaged and 60 were lost altogether, destroying the American belief that the bombers could successfully carry out missions unescorted by fighter planes.*

140

Q. In numerous air battles in the South Pacific during the early fall, the Japanese had lost planes in steadily increasing numbers. Why were the Japanese doing less and less well in air battles?

A. *They were able to replace planes well enough, but they were running short of experienced pilots. The very daring that from the start had marked the Japanese naval air force was now working against them, as the best pilots who took the most risks were shot down.*

Q. On November 1, the Marines made a landing on the island of Bougainville in the Solomons. It was defended by 60,000 Japanese army and navy personnel, but the Americans landed at a difficult stretch of beach held by a garrison of only 200, bringing in 14,000 Marines in a single day. Who was this island named for?

A. *The eighteenth-century French explorer Louis Alphonse de Bougainville. The native South American flowering shrub is also named for him.*

Q. Interior Secretary Harold Ickes said, "We can fuel all of the people some of the time, and fuel some of the people all of the time. But in a war we can't fuel all of the people all of the time." What was this punning statement made in connection with?

A. *The coal strikes of 1943, led by John L. Lewis, who was for a time almost as unpopular as Hitler. On November 1, Ickes had been ordered by Roosevelt to take over the mines and run them under the Solid Fuels Administration, a move that got 500,000 miners back to work on the third with a slight raise.*

141

Q. A former Peugeot automobile plant in France was sabotaged with bombs on November 5 by the French Resistance. The factory was regarded by the British as the third most important German-controlled installation in all of France. What were the Germans manufacturing there that made it so important?

A. *Tank turrets.*

Q. What Russian city was recaptured from the Germans on November 7 and why did the success rate a special radio broadcast by Stalin?

A. *Kiev, which had been the first major Russian city to fall to the Germans in the summer of 1941.*

Q. British Air Marshal Sir Arthur T. Harris began on November 18 what he called "The Battle of Berlin." This involved saturation bombing of the German capital over the coming four months, at a loss of 600 aircraft in over 9,000 sorties. Why did American military leaders tend to grit their teeth at the mention of Harris?

A. *They disliked his flair for publicity, to begin with, but more seriously were at odds with him on strategy, favoring the strategic bombing of particular targets.*

Q. A major invasion of two Japanese-held atolls in the Gilbert Islands was launched by American forces on November 20. The landing on Makin turned out to be more difficult than expected but in the end it was taken with relative ease in comparison with the near disaster that developed at Tarawa, 85 miles to the south. Which of the following went wrong at Tarawa?

    a.   The bombing of the Japanese garrison before the assault was ineffective

    b.   Freak tides prevented assault craft from getting to the beach itself over the exposed coral reefs

    c.   The Japanese proved to be better armed than expected

    d.   Communications between the assault forces and the command ships were confused

A.   *All of these things went wrong, but they were largely failures of preparation. The tide problem, for example, was a freak one, but a freak that commonly occurred. The battle at Tarawa was extremely costly, with the loss of 1,000 American lives as well as 2,000 wounded out of an invasion force of 14,000, all within a mere 36 hours. This battle proved to be the Pacific equivalent of the equally disastrous attempt to land at Dieppe in France earlier in the year. Lessons were learned that would not be forgotten.*

Q.   What marked the Allied conference in Teheran, Iran, from November 28 through December 1 as special?

A.   *It was the first time that Roosevelt, Churchill, and Stalin, together with their staffs, met in the same place. The decision tentatively agreed to by Roosevelt and Churchill to invade Europe in May of 1944 was firmly supported by Stalin. The Soviet leader also promised to enter the war against the Japanese once Germany had been defeated, should the Japanese still be fighting.*

Q.   In the United States there had been heated debate throughout the year concerning the drafting of men with dependent children. How was this finally resolved in early December?

A.   *A compromise passed by Congress and signed by Roosevelt put men who had become fathers before Pearl Harbor last on this list. This neatly avoided the sticky question of whether men were marrying and having children to avoid the draft.*

Q. What was a "patriotute"?

A. *This was a name coined for teenage girls who were GI groupies, willing to have sex with any man in uniform with the excuse that they might never come back.*

Q. At the end of December it was announced that General Eisenhower would be the Supreme Allied Commander in charge of the coming invasion of Europe, with British Air Marshal Sir Arthur Tedder as his deputy. Who was named to lead the British land forces for the invasion?

A. *General Montgomery. Numerous other command changes were made, but in parceling out these important assignments, the self-aggrandizing Air Marshal Harris was conspicuously overlooked. The Americans were now in charge in Europe as well as in the Pacific.*

Q. During November and December of 1943, how many convoys managed to cross the Atlantic completely unscathed?

    a. 56
    b. 63
    c. 78

A. *The answer is c. The total tonnage in lost ships during the two months was just over 300,000. A year earlier it had been 700,000 tons in an average month. The tide had turned in the Atlantic. The contest for the mainland of Europe was just beginning in the rain-swept winter hills of Italy, where progress was still marked off in miles per week.*

Part Six
1944: The Tide Turns

Q. By the end of the first week of January 1944, Soviet forces had crossed the border of what country in their attempt to drive the Germans out of the Soviet Union altogether?

A. *Poland, in terms of prewar frontiers. On a different front they also retook Kirovgrad in the Ukraine.*

Q. Late in December of 1943, the Marines had made a landing at Cape Gloucester on New Britain in the Solomon Islands. How far had they progressed by mid-January?

A. *They had advanced only a short distance beyond the original beachhead. Once again the Japanese were proving very tough to dislodge.*

Q. How were the attempts by the U.S. II Corps to cross the Rapido River 80 miles south of Rome and the Allied effort to bypass Monte Cassino further inland along the same line connected to the amphibious landing at Anzio, 35 miles south of Rome?

A. *Eisenhower had suggested that a surprise landing at Anzio would be easier than trying to bring sufficient troops and armor overland from the south. The efforts at the Rapido and Monte Cassino were intended to distract the Germans from the Anzio landing. But the forces at both sites were also supposed to break through and move up to catch the Germans in a trap between their forces and those that had landed at Anzio.*

Q. The Rapido River was no more than thirty feet wide at the point of attack. Why did General Fred L. Walker, the commander of the 36th Division, feel that the task was almost impossible?

A. *The very name of the Rapido River is part of the answer—its waters were extremely swift, as well as cold and deep. In addition, the banks of the river were at least four feet high and vertical. But what worried General Walker most was the fact that the Germans were so well entrenched on the other side of the river. He wrote in his diary that he could not recall any such attack succeeding in military history. And in fact it became a disaster, with infantrymen being shot out of the water like so many sitting ducks. The attack went on for two days, on the twentieth and twenty-first of January, with scarcely any success and terrible losses.*

Q. On the twenty-second 34,000 men were landed at Anzio, with only 13 killed. How fast were these troops able to move forward?

A. *The Germans quickly brought up several more divisions, and although the Allies landed a total of 69,000 by the twenty-ninth, they were unable to make much progress for two months. Since the crossing of the Rapido and the bypassing of Monte Cassino were both in trouble, the Allied plans were not working at all. Churchill caustically said of the Anzio landings, "I had hoped that we were hurling a wildcat onto the shore, but all we got was a stranded whale."*

1944: The Tide Turns

Q. The blockade of what Russian city had been totally dismantled by January 27?

A. *Leningrad. The siege that had begun in September of 1941 was over, but at least a million citizens of the city had died of the effects of malnutrition or outright starvation in the two years and five months it had lasted.*

Q. By February 4, American forces had taken Roi and Namur in the Marshall Islands from the Japanese. How long had this operation taken, from the first bombing raids to soften up the enemy positions?

    a.   One month
    b.   Two weeks
    c.   Five days

A. *The answer is c. The American forces had learned their lessons on island assaults and this operation was superbly orchestrated.*

Q. After they had made a final unsuccessful attempt to take the ancient monastery at Monte Cassino from the Germans, American troops were replaced by New Zealand and Indian troops commanded by General Sir Bernard Freyburg. What did Freyburg demand be done before any further attacks took place?

A. *That the monastery be bombed. It was believed that the Germans had occupied the fortresslike building, but in fact they had not. Several hundred citizens of the area and monks who lived in the monastery were killed as they were praying. What's more, the Germans then did occupy the ruins, which proved to be an even more formidable position than if the buildings had still been standing. By the fifteenth, Frey-*

burg's forces were in a far worse situation than when they took over on the twelfth.

Q. In mid-February, the Germans made several major attempts to drive the Allied forces from the Anzio beachhead. How successful was this effort?

A. *With their backs to the sea and despite heavy losses, the Allied troops dug in and hung on. In one of the grittiest actions in the course of the European war, their valiant defense of the beachhead persuaded the Germans that they could not dislodge the Allies.*

Q. In Norway on the twentieth, the Norwegian Resistance carried out British orders to sink a ferry carrying a highly significant cargo to Germany. What was the cargo?

A. *Heavy water essential to atomic research.*

Q. What did Hitler order in retaliation for the nonstop Allied bombing of Germany?

A. *New bombing attacks on London. Lasting from February 18 to 25, these raids were called the "Little Blitz." They were nowhere near the scale of the attacks during the Battle of Britain, however. The Luftwaffe was far too weakened to mount a major assault, and these raids were in fact an example of Hitler's rage getting the better of his military judgment.*

Q. The successful battle for Eniwetok in the last week of February put the Marshall Islands completely under U.S. control and opened a sea-lane 1,000 miles across the Pacific to the Mariana Islands. Of the Japanese garrison on the island there were only sixty-odd men left alive. How large had the garrison been?

A. *About 3,400. Similar losses had been sustained by the Japanese on other islands, the shame of surrender leading them to prefer death in battle. This would continue to be the case, and it would prove a double-edged sword for the Allies. The fierce Japanese resistance certainly led to increased Allied casualties, but the drain on Japanese manpower would tell against the Imperial forces in the long run.*

Q. What important role did the new P-51 Mustang play from the beginning of 1944 on?

A. *These fighter planes, superior to anything that had preceded them, were used as escorts for Allied bombers, and were instrumental in making Allied air raids more effective.*

Q. What were "paper bombs"?

A. *These were propaganda leaflets that the Allies dropped behind enemy lines in all theaters of war beginning in 1944; they were printed in appropriate languages and urged surrender.*

Q. Why was the Northrup P-61 fighter plane called the Black Widow?

A. *It was the first plane ever designed especially for night flying.*

Q. Why did the RAF fly a precision bombing strike against the prison at Amiens, France, on February 18?

A. *Their job was to knock down sections of the ramparts and create sufficient chaos to make it possible for the 258 inmates, most of whom were French Resistance fighters, to make their escape. The daring raid was a great success.*

Q. By March of 1944 an extremely volatile situation had developed in northern Burma. With the eventual goal of reopening the Burma Road, Nationalist Chinese forces under General Stilwell, British forces commanded by General Slim, and the Chindits commanded by Major General Orde Wingate, were all involved in movements on various fronts. Who were the Chindits?

A. *This was a guerrilla force, 3,000 strong and composed of British, Gurkha, and Burmese troops. They called themselves Chindits after the ceremonial lions that guarded the gates of Burmese temples. General Wingate was an eccentric man disliked by many in the British military but admired by Churchill and Lord Mountbatten, who was in overall command of land forces in Southeast Asia. Against the Italians in North Africa, Wingate had had some astonishing successes and was a charismatic "born leader" in the Lawrence of Arabia mold. Although Wingate would die in a plane crash on March 24, his fiercely loyal and brilliantly trained men were able to carry on as though he were still with them.*

Q. With all this activity, what did the Japanese commander in Burma decide to do?

A. *General Renya Mutaguchi decided on a preemptive counterattack into India at Kohima and Imphal, an operation code-named U-Go.*

Q. Name the winners of the New Hampshire presidential primary on March 14.

A. *Roosevelt won the Democratic primary even though he had not announced that he would run and most political insiders were convinced he would retire. Wendell Willkie also assumed Roosevelt would retire, and knew that his own victory in the Republican primary would have Roosevelt's secret blessing—the two men saw things much more similarly than did some of the potential Democratic candidates to succeed Roosevelt. But Willkie would soon come in fourth behind New York Governor Thomas Dewey, General MacArthur (who was being boosted by Republican conservatives even though he was in the Pacific fuming about being denied command of the entire Pacific war), and the "golden young man" of Wisconsin politics, Harold Stassen, who was also in the Pacific on Admiral Halsey's staff. Willkie would be a bitter man by the time he died on October 8 after a series of heart attacks.*

Q. In March of 1944, sixty B-25s were seriously damaged at the U.S.-held airport at Pompei, Italy. It was the worst setback in terms of lost military equipment that the Allies would suffer during the Italian campaign. How many German bombers had been sent against the airfield?

A. *None. Mount Vesuvius erupted, sending huge boulders flying across the countryside.*

Q. The German situation in Russia continued to deteriorate during the month of April, with Odessa taken on the tenth and the Germans forced to retreat in the Crimea on the twelfth. In the combined withdrawals, how many men were the Germans able to successfully evacuate?

    a.   15,000
    b.   24,000
    c.   67,000
    d.   101,000

A. *The combined total was 101,000, but large numbers of those escaping Odessa were wounded, where the fighting had been particularly fierce.*

Q. The code name for the real invasion of Europe across the Channel was Operation Overlord. What was Operation Fortitude?

A. *This was a fake invasion plan that would supposedly be commanded by General Patton, with the landing planned for the Pas de Calais area from Kent and Sussex directly across the Channel. Not only were elaborate fake radio messages contrived, but references to Operation Fortitude were also included in genuine messages. The Pas de Calais area would in fact have been the easiest place to attack, being the closest to England and having flat sandy beaches. But because it would be the easiest, and thus the area where the German buildup was most likely, Normandy was made the real target.*

Q. Field Marshal Gerd von Rundstedt was in command of the defense of Europe against the expected Allied attack, with Field Marshal Rommel directly under him. Did they agree on strategy?

A. *No. Rundstedt put more faith in the ability of the Luftwaffe to stall the invasion than Rommel did, and wanted to keep tank divisions pulled back but ready to push immediately toward whatever the eventual landing point of the Allies proved to be. Rommel wanted tanks brought forward to key positions. Hitler gave each man half a loaf when he should have listened to Rommel.*

Q. In New Guinea, American forces opened a major attack on Hollandia on April 22. How long did it take them to secure the area?

A. *Only a week. This was a very successful operation that caught the Japanese unprepared.*

Q. In preparation for D-Day, Allied bombers concentrated on French roads, bridges, and railway installations in order to make the movement of German forces as difficult as possible once the invasion began. But they dropped more bombs on the area to the rear of Pas de Calais than they did in the Normandy area. Why?

A. *Once again, this was part of the overall deception as to where the landing would actually take place. It succeeded in persuading Hitler that even if the invasion did come at Normandy, as he somewhat suspected, there would be a second invasion at Pas de Calais. His conviction that such a second invasion was planned led him to make a number of strategic mistakes in trying to hold the line against the Allies in June and July.*

Q. What was a DUK-W or "Duck"?

A. *"Ducks" were very versatile landing craft that had been built on half-ton-truck chassis. With a watertight hull, a propeller, and a rudder, they were almost as maneuverable in the water as on land. During the invasion of Sicily, 1,000 of the vehicles had been used; at Normandy twice that number were involved in the landings.*

Q. How many ships and landing craft were assembled on the British coast in the weeks before D-Day?

A. *The total number was 6,483, of which more than 4,000 were landing craft.*

Q. The garrisons on the Indian-Burmese border at Imphal and Kohima managed to hold out against larger Japanese forces due to air drops of food and supplies. Why were the Japanese beginning to weaken seriously by mid-May?

A. *Despite repeated requests, they had received no supplies at all from the rear. By the time the Japanese gave up and retreated at the end of the third week of June, their troops had been reduced to eating grasses and slugs. More than two thirds of the original force of 85,000 were lost.*

Q. On May 17, after making a three-week "end run" through mountainous jungle terrain, "Merrill's Marauders," as they called themselves, captured an important airfield near the railhead at Myitkyina in Northeast Burma. This operation, conceived by General Stilwell, had been regarded as impossible by almost everyone but Stilwell and Colonel Frank D. Merrill himself. What was it about Merrill that made the success of this operation even more astonishing?

A. *Merrill had checked himself out of the hospital, where he had been recuperating from a heart attack, to lead his men on the trek through the jungle. Because of early monsoon rains, they had had to crawl on their hands and knees at some points to get over the mountainous territory. Riven by malaria and dysentery, they took the airport from the flabbergasted Japanese, and troops and supplies were immediately flown in.*

Q. Why did the Japanese gather a large proportion of their fleet in the Sulu Sea in mid-May?

A. *They were determined to protect the Mariana Islands from attack by U.S. forces, having correctly assumed that that would be the next target. The defense was known as A-Go.*

1944: The Tide Turns

Q. Polish troops finally took what Italian hill town on May 18?

A. *Monte Cassino. It had taken a succession of troops from the United States, New Zealand, and India, and finally Free Polish forces, nearly five months to break the German hold there. Also by mid-May, British, French, Canadian, and U.S. forces were gradually succeeding in pushing the Germans back in the Liri Valley, but the casualty toll was high.*

Q. What new German weapon did Polish resistance fighters manage to get hold of at the end of the third week of May?

A. *A V-2 test rocket that landed 100 miles from Warsaw. Hiding it from the Germans for the next two months, they finally managed to get parts of it flown to England in late July.*

Q. In 1939, the U.S. government had about 1 million employees. How many did it have by mid-1944?

    a. More than twice as many
    b. Three times as many
    c. Nearly four times as many

A. *The answer is* c. *Government employees now numbered 3.8 million.*

Q. In 1940 there had been 100,000 Americans employed in the aircraft industry. How many times as many worked in the industry by 1944?

A. *Twenty times as many, or 2 million.*

Q. Many states repealed their child-labor laws during World War II. Is this true or false?

A. *True. By mid-1944, at least 3 million twelve- to seventeen-year-olds were engaged in paid war work.*

Q. A photographer from the serviceman's magazine *Yank* got permission to photograph a pretty girl working in an aircraft plant in Bakersfield, California. After the picture appeared, she was offered some small modeling jobs by a local photographer. Who was she?

A. *Her name was Norma Jean Baker Dougherty, but it would become Marilyn Monroe.*

Q. Below is a list of major male movie stars. Connect each name with the appropriate wartime activity in the right-hand column.

a.	Henry Fonda	1.	4-F because of punctured eardrums, made movies
b.	Ronald Reagan	2.	In the Navy
c.	Frank Sinatra	3.	Made training films in Army Air Force as captain
d.	John Wayne	4.	Conscientious objector, in Medical Corps
e.	Lew Ayres	5.	Piloted twenty bomber missions over Germany, rose to colonel
f.	Glenn Ford	6.	In the Marines
g.	James Stewart	7.	Made war movies

A. *a,2; b,3; c,1; d,7; e,4; f,6; g,5*

Q. Name the two female Hollywood stars who virtually abandoned their careers to entertain American troops.

A. *Joan Blondell and Marlene Dietrich. Blondell hurt her career by taking so much time off. Dietrich, who was extremely anti-Nazi from the start, had refused a personal order from Hitler to return to Germany in the mid-thirties. Her impression on the troops was immense and in later years when she made her concert tours there were always men in the audience with tears in their eyes who had heard her sing at the front.*

Q. Field Marshal Sir Harold Alexander, the overall commander of Allied forces in Italy, ordered General Mark Clark to continue to drive northward to the east of Rome to encircle the retreating German Tenth Army. But Clark issued a different order to his American troops. What was it and why did he do it?

A. *Clark ordered his forces to march on Rome, which he wanted to have the glory of taking. He and Alexander had been consistently at odds, Clark feeling the British were too cautious. He also suspected that the British planned to march into Rome on their own. Not only did Clark's action allow the Germans to regroup, but the American arrival in Rome on June 4 was an anticlimax—still fearful of the Germans, the people of Rome stayed quietly at home.*

Q. D-Day was supposed to be June 4. Why was it delayed?

A. *The weather was so bad that it would have made both a sea landing and the dropping of paratroopers on the French coast impossible. Some of the invading fleet from the more distant ports along the English coast had actually started out and had to be called back.*

Q. Gold, Juno, and Sword were three of the five code names for what?

A. *The landing areas along a 60-mile stretch of the Normandy coast. The other two were Utah and Omaha.*

Q. How many Allied planes had been massed to provide support for the D-Day invasion?

   a. 8,000
   b. 10,000
   c. 12,000

A. *The answer is* c, of which 5,000 were fighter planes.

Q. There were over 4,600 American casualties on the Normandy beaches on D-Day. Where did the great majority of them occur?

A. *At Omaha beach. There was great difficulty in getting tanks and artillery on shore; the best of the defending German divisions was located there, and the topography, with surrounding cliffs and steep dunes, heavily favored the Germans. One fifth of the total landing force of 23,000 men were killed or wounded at the five landing points on D-Day, but in fact that was a considerably lower casualty figure than the Allies had feared.*

Q. Once the landing at Normandy had been effected, command of the Allied land forces was passed to General Montgomery, who had been involved in the planning since January. Why was it a British and not an American general in this position, since the largest number of ground forces were in fact U.S. troops?

A. *It was part of the agreement that had made Eisenhower Supreme Commander. Beyond that, Montgomery's experi-*

1944: The Tide Turns

ence against Rommel in North Africa gave him the greatest amount of expertise in facing German armored divisions.

Q. In the first raid on Japan itself since the Doolittle attack on Tokyo in 1941, American bombers stationed in China attacked Yawata on the island of Kyushu, on June 15. What kind of bombers made this raid?

A. *Superfortress B-29s. These superbly designed planes, with great range and large bomb capacity, were the foremost triumph of American war manufacturing. In factories all across the United States, more than 16 million people played some part, however small, in building these planes that ultimately won the war in the Pacific and were of enormous importance in Europe as well.*

Q. What came crashing down on England for the first time on June 13?

A. *A V-1 rocket. These rockets could travel 400 miles per hour and carried 2,000 pounds of explosives in their nose cones.*

Q. How many V-1s did the Germans launch against England between June 13 and September 8?

    a. 8,000
    b. 12,000
    c. 18,000

A. *The answer is* c.

Q. How many of the V-1s were the British able to shoot down or explode before they landed?

The World War II Quiz Book

A. *About half were shot down by a defensive force that operated under the name Operation Crossbow. In early August,
the pilot of an experimental British jet was able to catch up
with an incoming V-1, slip a wing tip underneath the rocket
and flip it over.*

Q. Who was given authority over the liberated areas of France?

A. *General de Gaulle's Provisional Government of the Repub-
lic of France. This was a major victory for de Gaulle.*

Q. What was "The Great Marianas Turkey Shoot"?

A. *This was the name given by American GIs to the June 19
battle in the Philippine Sea that devastated Japanese forces
with small cost to American forces. Everything that could go
wrong for the Japanese did, including the loss of two carriers and nearly 300 planes. The Japanese had planned to
use their base at Guam as a standby staging area during the
battle, but the United States had struck Guam from the air
before the battle and was to strike it again as planes from the
sinking carriers tried to land there. Not wanting to lose face,
the Japanese troops on Guam did not inform their superiors
of their weakened situation.*

Q. On the island of Biak off New Guinea, American forces
were faced with a messy, time-consuming problem in bringing to a conclusion an invasion that had been expected to go
fairly easily. This was because of the Japanese use of a
natural feature of the island. What was it?

A. *Caves. This was a problem the Allies would encounter for
the rest of the war at numerous sites. Although surrounded
and without food, pockets of Japanese soldiers would refuse*

*to surrender, forcing the Allies to kill them with grenades
and fire bombs where they lay hidden. Some Japanese troops
hid out in such caves for years, in a few cases even decades,
after the war was over. It took from June until the end of
July to finally root out the Japanese on Biak.*

Q. After three weeks in France, the Allies took their first major
prize, seizing control of Cherbourg on the twenty-seventh of
June. Why was this a particularly important success?

A. *As a large port Cherbourg would give the Allies far easier
access to the Continent once it was cleared of mines and
made operational. Even though the Allies had by now managed to land well over 600,000 troops by way of Normandy,
it had been a costly operation, with a casualty rate of more
than 10 percent.*

Q. What took place at Bretton Woods, New Hampshire, during
the first three weeks of July that would have wide impact on
the postwar world?

A. *An economic conference involving most of the free nations of
the world, forty-four in all, which established the concept of
an International Monetary Fund and laid the groundwork
for postwar reconstruction.*

Q. In order to fight their way through to the open land of Brittany, the Allied soldiers had to fight their way through what
was called *bocage* country. What feature of the landscape
made this a particularly dangerous and difficult passage?

A. *Hedges, but not just ordinary hedges. Many had been
planted as far back as the first few centuries A.D. They were*

163

high, virtually impenetrable, and turned the roadways into something resembling corridors in a maze.

Q. Even though he was a civilian, Charles Lindbergh shot down a Japanese fighter plane in 1944. True or false?

A. *This is true. He had been brought out to the Pacific as an adviser to help train pilots to fly the new P-38s, and on one training mission a Japanese fighter came dead at his plane. The fact that this had happened was kept a secret until after the war because of his civilian status.*

Q. Using pierced-steel mats dropped by parachute from U.S. planes, 100 unskilled workers could construct what in 90 hours?

A. *A 3,000-foot-long, 150-foot-wide runway in areas that had just been conquered. These runways were used particularly in the South Pacific and Southeast Asia.*

Q. As the island of Saipan came under control of the U.S. forces in the Marianas, what did thousands of Japanese civilians and surviving troops do on July 9?

A. *At the 800-foot-high Morubi bluffs, women and children threw themselves off, while soldiers blew themselves up with their own grenades, believing they would be put to death by the Americans anyway. This mass suicide brought the number of Japanese dead in the battle for Saipan to at least 40,000. For the Americans, the losses were the worst yet in the Pacific: 3,000 dead and 13,000 wounded.*

Q. Who wrote the following words on July 9: "1600 Pennsylvania Avenue is a nice address but I'd rather not move in through the back door—or any other door at sixty."

1944: The Tide Turns

A. *Harry Truman wrote these words to his daughter, Margaret, only ten days before the Democratic Convention convened in Chicago. They make clear that he knew he was being considered as a running mate for Roosevelt, and in addition that he realized Roosevelt was ill. There are dozens of conflicting stories about the backstage maneuvering that led to the choice of Truman over the sitting vice-president, Henry Wallace (whom many important Democrats wanted to get rid of), and former senator and Supreme Court justice James "Jimmy" Byrnes, who had become virtually an "assistant president" to Roosevelt. Much of the confusion was clearly created by Roosevelt himself, who told everybody something different about his own personal choice. But it was Truman who was nominated in Chicago—if Roosevelt had not wanted him, it would not have happened.*

Q. What island that the Japanese had seized right after Pearl Harbor did American forces invade on the twenty-first of July?

A. *Guam, where bitter fighting would last until August 10, resulting in 7,000 American casualties, including 1,500 dead. The Japanese force of nearly 10,000 would be virtually wiped out.*

Q. Why did Colonel Claus von Stauffenberg leave a briefcase under a conference table at Rastenburg Fortress on July 20?

A. *It contained a bomb and was part of a plot to kill Hitler. Stauffenberg was a disabled officer of the old school, an aristocrat with a cavalry background, just the sort of military man Hitler had always distrusted. After leaving the bomb, Stauffenberg flew to Berlin to carry out the rest of the conspiracy, which would have involved putting military men in all leadership posts. The bomb went off, but it had been*

165

moved just enough so that Hitler was protected from the main force of the blast and was only slightly injured. Stauffenberg and a number of other conspirators were shot that night, hundreds of others over the next few weeks. Hitler suspected that the wounded Rommel and his replacement, Field Marshal Gunther von Kluge, were in on the plot, but although they had known about it they had done nothing to actively encourage it—or discourage it. The incident did have the effect of further destabilizing Hitler psychologically.

Q. On July 21 Marine veterans of Guadalcanal landed on two separate beaches on Guam, which had been under Japanese control since December 10, 1941. They found a sign on one of the beaches that said WELCOME MARINES. Who had left it?

A. *U.S. Navy underwater demolition teams who had been combing the beaches for mines.*

Q. On July 25, near Saint-Lô in Normandy, 4,700 tons of bombs were dropped on German lines in an area only 7,000 yards wide and 3,000 yards deep. What tragic consequences did a shift in the breeze that carried smoke backward from the target area have?

A. *It misled some Allied bombers into dropping bombs on General Omar Bradley's land forces massed just to the northeast of the German positions, causing several hundred casualties.*

Q. Name the American correspondent with Bradley's forces who was right in the middle of the mistaken bombing and reported the horror of the American soldiers as the bombs rained down.

1944: The Tide Turns

A. *Ernie Pyle, the most famous of all the war correspondents during World War II. Pyle identified strongly with the ordinary soldier and told far more truths about their fears, sorrows, and wrenched guts than the military brass would have liked.*

Q. The bombing of the German lines at Saint-Lô was part of the plan known as Operation Cobra, which called for Bradley's forces to open the way for a fresh force—the head of the Cobra—to strike through into Brittany and the rest of France. What American general was in command of the head of the Cobra?

A. *That tough-as-nails old warrior General George Patton, who led his Third Army across France at breakneck speed starting on August 2.*

Q. On July 23, the town of Pskov fell to Soviet forces. What made this a landmark event?

A. *It was the last major German stronghold in the Soviet Union, adding to Hitler's depressed mood.*

Q. Why did Roosevelt fly to Honolulu to meet with General MacArthur and Admiral Nimitz in late July?

A. *MacArthur's fury at the navy's repeated resistance to his ideas about how the Pacific war should be fought was coming to a boil. Nimitz and the Joint Chiefs of Staff had wanted to bypass the Philippines and attack Formosa, which they felt would provide a better base for a final assault on Japan. But that would postpone the fulfillment of MacArthur's personal promise to return and liberate the Philippines. MacArthur was in a fairly strong position since the campaign to*

*retake all of New Guinea, which he had directed with con-
siderable strategic brilliance, was now coming to an end. To
Roosevelt, whom he disliked both personally and politically
(he had been very much against many New Deal policies),
he pointedly said that the United States had a moral obli-
gation to the people of the Philippines, and that if Roosevelt
shunted it aside, the American people would rightly take him
to task for it. That was not what Roosevelt wanted with the
election coming up, but it was hardly something MacArthur
needed to point out to the most successful politician in American history. Roosevelt agreed to go after the Philippines
first, but it took another month to persuade the navy to go
along with that strategy.*

Q. Why, in the summer of 1944, did Soviet forces come to a
halt short of liberating Warsaw from the Germans?

A. *They claimed that they needed to replenish supplies and rest
their troops, but postwar analysts generally believe that Stalin's real desire was to allow the Germans to further debil-
itate the Polish people, making it easier for the Soviets to
co-opt the country behind the eventual Iron Curtain.*

Q. What Italian city did the Allies finally enter on August 6?

A. *Florence. It had been almost eleven months since the Allies
first landed on the mainland of Italy.*

Q. Guam was almost fully in American hands by the tenth of
August, although some Japanese were still hiding in the
jungle. When did the last Japanese soldier on Guam finally
surrender?

A. *In 1972; he returned to Japan as a kind of real-life Rip Van
Winkle.*

1944: The Tide Turns

Q. What landing did Churchill go to witness from the deck of a destroyer in mid-August?

A. *The invasion of Southern France between Toulon and Cannes. Originally, it had been believed that the Allies would be able to enter what Churchill liked to call "the soft underbelly of Europe" through Italy, but the Italian campaign had lasted far longer than expected.*

Q. The second greatest battle of its kind in World War II had begun in Northern France in the first week of August and was now drawing to a close at the Falaise Gap. What kind of battle was it?

A. *Ten Allied tank divisions had faced off against ten German tank divisions, second only to the massive Soviet-German confrontation at Kursk the previous year. But this battle, which raged for two weeks, was a much more close-up, tank-versus-tank, engagement. It was also different in that air power played a vital part, ceaselessly bombarding the escape routes of the Germans over an 800-square-mile area, whereas at Kursk air power had been rendered virtually useless, and the battle was won because of the Russian minefields and antitank guns. By the time the battle was over at Falaise on the seventeenth, the bombing from the air had made the town itself impassable—there were no streets left.*

Q. Field Marshal Kluge committed suicide on the eighteenth. Was this simply because he had failed to hold the Allied forces at Falaise and had been dismissed by Hitler?

A. *No. He realized that Hitler suspected him of being a part of the July assassination plot and that only victory would have sufficed to save him. To return to Berlin now would be to stand trial for treason.*

Q. Montgomery's 21st Army Group and the American First Army closed in rapidly on Paris, and were joined by French troops brought up to share in the honor of liberating the city. Within the city General Choltitz refused to carry out Hitler's order to do what?

A. *To destroy the city before the Allies arrived. Dietrich von Choltitz had been the general in charge of the destruction of both Rotterdam and Sevastapol, but he could not bring himself to set Paris ablaze for no good reason and instead surrendered to the Allies.*

Q. Despite the presence of holdout German soldiers, who returned to Paris to join a victory parade on August 26?

A. *General de Gaulle, who then gave a speech in which he spoke as though the French, and the French alone, were responsible for the liberation of their country.*

Q. The capital of what other Western European nation was liberated on September 3?

A. *Belgium. With the German collapse in France, the retaking of Brussels and southern and central Belgium posed little problem. But the coast, and particularly the great port of Antwerp, was still strongly held, which would add to the difficulty of supplying the vast Allied armies now on the Continent.*

Q. What kind of regulations were made less stringent in Britain in the first week of September, and why was this ironic?

A. *Blackout and related civil-defense measures. This was made ironic by the fact that the first V-2 rocket, which of course needed no lights to guide it, landed on London on the eighth.*

Q. On the tenth an armistice was signed between two countries that had been at war with one another, allied to Germany, at war with one another again, on and off for the past five years. Name them.

A. *Finland and the Soviet Union. This agreement called upon Finland to make reparations to the Soviet Union, accompanied by a restoration of 1940 boundaries.*

Q. After bombardment from both sea and air, a major French port was taken from the 12,000 German defenders in twenty-four hours on September 12. Name it.

A. *Le Havre.*

Q. The armistice signed between the Allies and Romania, which had already declared war on Germany, brought the release of more than 1,000 Allied troops. What kind of troops were they?

A. *Airmen who had parachuted or crashed behind enemy lines in the previous three years.*

Q. Operation Market Garden was an Allied plan devised by Montgomery to open another route into Germany. It involved dropping paratroopers into what country on September 17?

A. *Holland. If the German-controlled river and canal bridges on the border could be taken, there would be a clear route into Germany itself. The success of the plan depended upon land troops connecting up with the paratroopers. But the German forces were considerably stronger than expected, and despite success in some areas, more than 6,000 British paratroopers were taken prisoner near Arnhem, with another 1,000 killed. The remainder of the 10,000 paratroopers were evacuated across the Rhine River in small boats.*

Q. The Germans surrendered the French port of Calais at the very end of September. Was this small city taken by British, American, Canadian, or Free French troops?

A. *The Canadians were responsible for this important conquest.*

Q. The revolt of the Polish resistance led by General Tadeusz Bor-Komarowski that had begun in August was finally crushed by the Germans on October 2. How many Poles had died in this brave but ultimately futile uprising?

A. *At least 200,000.*

Q. What was the special significance of Allied attacks around Aachen in early October?

A. *This was the first place the Allies broke through the Siegfried Line, Germany's answer to the French Maginot Line.*

Q. Two members of Hitler's staff visited Field Marshal Rommel, still recovering from his wounds, on the fourteenth of October. What was the fiendish choice they offered him?

A. *A choice between a trial for treason or suicide. Hitler was convinced Rommel had been involved in the July plot to assassinate him, and wanted him out of the way in case of future rebellions from within the army. But because of Rommel's enormous popularity within Germany and his standing even among the Allies, it was important to Hitler not to allow it to be known that he was behind Rommel's death. He thus sweetened the deal by promising that if Rommel killed himself with poison thoughtfully brought along by his staff members, there would be no reprisals against his family and Rommel himself would be given a state funeral. With no real choice, Rommel took the poison, and for once Hitler kept his word.*

Q. By what nickname was Iva (Ikuko) Toguri, an American citizen of Japanese heritage, called during the war in the Pacific?

A. *"Tokyo Rose" was what the GIs called this woman who broadcast Japanese propaganda in English. The GIs thought she was a lot of fun, but after the war she was tried for treason, and spent six years in prison despite her adamant insistence that she had been caught in Tokyo visiting a sick relative at the time of Pearl Harbor. After twenty years of contesting her conviction, she was finally given a presidential pardon by Gerald Ford.*

Q. Whose legs were so famous that they even got painted on the sides of bombers?

A. *Betty Grable was the number-one GI pinup of World War II, closely followed by Rita Hayworth.*

Q. After bombing and shelling the island of Leyte in the Philippines for four days, MacArthur's forces made a rapid and very successful landing on the east coast of the island on the twentieth of October. Photographs of MacArthur wading ashore that afternoon would appear on the front pages of newspapers around the world. Why didn't he come ashore on a landing craft?

A. *He tried to, but there were so many troops coming ashore that a beachmaster, not realizing who was aboard, waved the boat off, yelling, "Let 'em walk!" MacArthur was furious, but turned the incident into a public-relations coup by wading ashore at every landing from then on. By that evening, there were 136,000 troops on Leyte, and the Japanese had withdrawn to previously prepared defense further inland. MacArthur made an emotional radio speech to the Philippine people announcing his promised return.*

Q. As the Leyte landings were taking place, what was the Japanese Navy doing?

A. *A Combined Fleet was sailing toward the Philippines to take on the American forces. It included the two largest warships in the world, the superbattleships* Musashi *and the* Yamato, *in a force commanded by Admiral Takeo Kurita aboard the heavy cruiser* Atago. *A second group of ships was under the command of Admiral Teiji Nishimura, and a third group under Admiral Jisaburo Ozawa planted itself 200 miles off Luzon. This third group, however, was made up in part of carriers without planes and was intended as bait to lure American ships away from the Leyte.*

Q. Because the Japanese had changed codes and used false messages during the buildup, the U.S. fleet was unaware of the size of the incoming force. How did they find out what was happening?

A. *Two patrolling U.S. submarines came upon Kurita's force, radioed its whereabouts in the Palawan passage and then attacked, managing to sink the* Atago, *thus forcing Kurita to transfer to the* Yamato. *Two other heavy cruisers were also sunk.*

Q. In the battle to come, the Japanese were hampered by a lack of what element of their usual fighting strength?

A. *Air cover. They were seriously low on planes and pilots. Half of the force that was supposed to defend the Philippines from the air had been shot down defending Formosa, where the United States had made recent attacks.*

Q. Because of the lack of planes, volunteer pilots had been ordered to make what kind of attacks on American ships?

A. *Kamikaze suicide attacks. Planes with bombs strapped under the wings deliberately crashed into the decks of American ships. The name* kamikaze *referred to the Divine Wind that had played havoc with an invading Mongol fleet at the end of the thirteenth century. The first of these attacks turned the carrier* Princeton *into an inferno.*

Q. Torpedo after torpedo was launched at the enormous bulk of the *Musashi,* but the ship seemed to be able to absorb anything that hit it. Its crew in fact believed it to be unsinkable. Did that turn out to be true?

A. *No. The battleship was so badly damaged that it was ordered to retreat to an island or atoll where it could be beached. But it sank during the night. The* Yamato *was also damaged, but survived.*

Q. In fact, the *Yamato* ought to have been sunk also. What prevented that from happening?

175

A. *Admiral Halsey took the bait offered by the planeless car-riers and sailed off to attack them. His forces wreaked havoc on the decoy force, but in the meantime Kurita's ships were engaged in a huge battle with the American forces off Leyte. More kamikaze hits were made on American ships and it was only the American air attacks that prevented a debacle. Admiral Halsey received a request for help and turned back. But he knew he could not get there in time, and lamented afterward that he had not stayed and finished off the decoy fleet. As for Kurita, he too made a mistake, thinking the U.S. air power was greater than it was. He retreated; if he had joined up with Admiral Nishimura's forces they might well have been able to overwhelm the U.S. ships protecting Leyte. The Imperial Navy would never recover from the Battle of Leyte, but both Kurita and Halsey were severely criticized for their actions.*

Q. On November 6, Roosevelt was elected president for the fourth time. Was his share of the popular vote higher or lower than in 1932 when he was first elected?

A. *It was higher in raw numbers due to population increases, but at 53 percent it was his lowest share in all his elections. Even so, he carried thirty-six states. The campaign slogan "Don't change horses in mid-stream" had hit home with the American people. The war was going well and even many people who thought Roosevelt had been in office too long preferred to deal with the devil they knew rather than a candidate like Thomas Dewey who was utterly innocent of foreign-policy experience.*

Q. Why was the planned mission of Halsey's Third Fleet against Japan postponed on November 10?

A. *Because MacArthur's troops on Leyte were being bom-barded daily by Japanese planes, the bulk of the remaining force having been directed to the Philippines. In addition, Japanese troops were being landed on Leyte by sea at a fast pace. Halsey's ships were needed to gain control of both situations.*

Q. What do the following aircraft have in common?

    a. Heinkel HE-178
    b. Messerschmitt ME-202
    c. Meteor
    d. Nakajima Kikka
    e. Bell XP-59B

A. *All were jet aircraft. Although the Germans got there first with the Heinkel HE-178, in 1939, they had serious problems with it. Most of these aircraft were not flying, even as experimental models, until late in the war, and none was being produced in sufficient numbers to have any important effect on the outcome of the war. If Hitler had had sufficient jets a year earlier, however, it might well have been impossible to invade Europe until the Allies were able to catch up in jet technology.*

Q. What was launched from bases in the Mariana Islands on November 24?

A. *The first of many massive B-29 raids on Tokyo.*

Q. In mid-September Hitler had announced at a meeting of his military leaders that it was his intention to mount a massive December counterattack against the Allies through the Ardennes region of Belgium and Luxembourg that the Germans had swept through with such ease in 1940. His aim was to retake the port of Antwerp, thus cutting off the Allies' main supply route. He maintained that if the Allies could be driven back and stalled in France, the bombardment of both their positions and of Britain with V-2 rockets would force the Allies to at the very least make a peace agreement favorable to Germany. What did his military leaders think of this proposal?

A. *Most of them were by then convinced that simply defending Germany from invasion was a formidable task, and that a counterattack would only forestall the inevitability of that task. They were simply astonished at the proposal.*

Q. Given their feeling that a counteroffensive could not ultimately succeed, why did Hitler's generals go along with it?

A. *One thing Hitler said made sense to them: the idea that a more favorable peace could eventually be arranged, with or without Hitler's participation. They were greatly concerned by the call for "unconditional surrender" that Roosevelt and Churchill had made after their Casablanca conference in January of 1943. Roosevelt had insisted upon the use of this term, which had first been used by General Grant during the Civil War, because he did not want to see a repeat of the messy peace agreements that followed World War I. But the idea frightened the German generals, who saw it as tantamount to losing the national identity of Germany.*

Q. As the Germans began to rebuild their forces and put them in place for the December counteroffensive, did the Allies have any idea of what was occurring?

A. *Very little. The Germans operated with great secrecy and what hints there were in Allied intelligence reports were ignored by both the British and the American high command. They were convinced they had the Germans on the run and that with better weather and ample supplies they would be able to finish things off quickly in the early spring.*

Q. There were some Allied officers who were nervous. The commander of the eighty-five-mile-long Ardennes Line, with headquarters at Bastogne, was one of them. General Troy Middleton even voiced his concern to General Bradley, saying that he felt the troops defending the line were too few in number. What did Bradley reply?

A. *He said not to worry, the Germans certainly wouldn't be coming through there.*

Q. How many troops did the Germans manage to muster behind the Ardennes Line?

    a. 200,000
    b. 250,000
    c. 300,000

A. *The Germans mustered 300,000 men backed up by massive artillery and nearly 1,000 tanks.*

Q. One of the panzer divisions was the SS 12th, made up of recruits from the Hitler Youth Movement. Their division had been formed in 1943 when its troops were seventeen years old. Was this a sign of a desperate shortage of manpower?

A. *There was certainly a manpower crisis, but these teenagers, who had known nothing but Hitler's rule, and had been indoctrinated over a ten-year period, were among the bravest, best, and most fanatical of Hitler's troops. They had already proved themselves in Normandy and were put at the forefront of the attack.*

Q. The German attack came on the night of December 16 with earthshaking bombing and shelling of Allied positions. Under an overcast sky illuminated by intense searchlights, the German land forces moved forward before dawn. What did the SS troops do with American soldiers who surrendered in the early fighting?

A. *Lined them up and shot them. One of these incidents quickly became known among the GIs up and down the front and had the unintended effect of galvanizing them into stronger resistance. Hitler himself had ordered that early prisoners be executed in order to spread terror among the Allies, but the ploy backfired.*

Q. The struggle that ensued was officially named the Battle of the Ardennes. But it very quickly came to be called the Battle of the Bulge. Why?

A. *This name was started by American GIs, who saw that the German advance was bulging out toward them from the middle. The name was quickly picked up by frontline journalists and stuck forever.*

Q. Despite heavy losses and panic among civilians in Belgium, the Allies quickly picked themselves up and set about blocking the German advance. Individual battalions and even small corps of troops responded with enormous courage and just plain common sense, dropping back just enough to find a position that could be held and then holding it. General Patton managed to get three divisions on their feet, turned around in the opposite direction, and in the thick of the battle in only three days—an undertaking only a Patton could have managed. General Montgomery kept an extremely cool head, convinced that the German forces would wear themselves down in what was clearly a desperate measure. And, in a famous one word message, General Anthony C. MacAuliffe replied to a German demand for the surrender of Bastogne. What did he say?

A. *"Nuts." The full note read, "To the German Commander: Nuts! The American Commander."*

Q. What happened on the twenty-third that ensured the Allies would be able to turn back the German counteroffensive?

A. *The overcast, misty weather finally broke, meaning that Allied planes could be brought in to attack the German ground forces. There would be vicious fighting in many sectors for weeks to come, but day by day the German bulge would be belted in notch by notch.*

Q. By the end of December, the battle for Leyte in the Philippines was fundamentally over, with 15,000 American casualties and a Japanese death toll approaching 70,000. As General Marshall contemplated these horrific figures in Washington, a report was presented to him on the twenty-ninth of December that gave hope for a conclusion to the war in 1945. What were the contents of this report?

A. *It was from General Groves, in charge of the Manhattan Project, and it gave assurances that an atomic bomb would be ready to be used by August 1 of 1945.*

Part Seven
1945: Victory

Q. On January 1, 1945, nearly 800 German planes attacked Allied airfields in the north of France as well as Belgium and Holland. The surprise attack knocked out almost 300 Allied planes while the Germans lost only two thirds as many. Why then was this more of a setback for the Luftwaffe than for the Allied air forces?

A. *In Britain and the United States, the production of planes was at a peak, whereas in Germany Allied bombing of factories had brought plane production to new lows. What's more, the Germans were running short of trained pilots. Many of the pilots in this operation were extremely inexperienced and in some cases managed to shoot one another down.*

Q. On January 7 the fleet under way to Luzon, the main island of the Philippines, was attacked by kamikazes, which put two battleships out of action and damaged a number of other ships. Why was there no air cover to fight off the kamikazes?

A. *Halsey's carriers were nearby but bad weather prevented them from getting their planes off the deck with ease and would have made it almost impossible to land them again. The kamikazes, which came from land bases on Luzon, were not, of course, concerned with landing conditions.*

Q. In early January there was a disagreement between the Soviet Union and both the United States and Britain concerning Poland. What was it?

A. *The Soviets recognized what was known as the Lublin Committee in Poland as the provisional government of that country. There were supposedly only three communists among the committee's fifteen members, but the group would eventually agree to a new border with the Soviet Union that ceded 40,000 square miles of prewar Poland to the Soviets. This was exactly what the United States and Britain were afraid would happen and they continued to recognize the Polish Government in Exile, based in London, as the legitimate Polish authority.*

Q. The U.S. landings on Luzon were initiated on the ninth of January, ten days earlier than originally planned. How many Japanese troops were on Luzon?

    a. 170,000
    b. 260,000
    c. 310,000

A. *The answer is b; they were split into two main groups, with 150,000 in the north and another 110,000 in the vicinity of Manila.*

Q. The Soviets began a new push forward in Poland on the twelfth. In doing so, were they going against U.S. and British wishes?

A. *No. Churchill had specifically requested Stalin to begin a new offensive in spite of his concerns about the Lublin Committee. He felt that a new Soviet effort would help take some of the weight off the shoulders of the Allied forces in the Ardennes, where fighting was still continuing.*

Q. On the seventeenth of January the last of the German pockets of resistance were overcome in Warsaw. In what condition was the city?

A. *It was at this point the most heavily damaged city in Europe.*

Q. Why was General Slim pleased that Japanese troops were moving to counterattack Allied troops that had crossed the Irrawaddy River north of Mandalay in Burma?

A. *Because a larger Allied force was getting ready to attack from the south, and the Japanese forces were now being split.*

Q. Name the major South Pacific air-force base that was partially reclaimed for the first time since January of 1942 on January 25?

A. *Clark Field on Luzon.*

Q. By the end of the month, Allied forces had in several places crossed into Germany, more than regaining the ground lost in the Battle of the Bulge. How many American casualties had the campaign cost?

A. *Nearly 77,000 out of a total of 81,000, the heaviest losses in U.S. history in a single campaign. But Germany had lost more than 100,000, making its manpower situation even more grave at a time when thousands of fresh American troops were arriving in Europe almost daily.*

Q. Beginning on the fourth of February, Stalin was host to Roosevelt and Churchill at Yalta in the Crimea. Churchill, with political problems looming at home, and a gravely tired Roosevelt were not at their best. They extracted a promise from Stalin that there would be free elections in Eastern Europe, but did not nail it down properly. On numerous issues they gave in to Stalin or left matters hanging. But they got the promise Roosevelt wanted most. What was it?

A. *That the Soviets would join the war against Japan once Germany was defeated.*

Q. In Greece, negotiations following the defeat of the Germans led to an amnesty between the newly constituted Greek government and what group of Greek partisans?

A. *The Greek Communist party. The Communists were required to turn in their arms, but would cause endless trouble in the postwar world, even though Stalin kept to a promise made at Yalta not to intervene with force.*

Q. The Soviet forces took more than 100,000 German prisoners in what Eastern European capital in mid-February?

A. *Budapest. Hungary had been a hapless ally to Germany since the fall of 1940. Soon it would be behind the Iron Curtain.*

Q. From February 13 through 15, Allied planes, mostly from the RAF but with some American support, bombed what German city in a raid that would cause a storm of controversy?

A. *Dresden, which was regarded as the most beautiful city in Germany and was home to the foremost porcelain factories in Europe. After the event there were bitter arguments as to whether the city had any military significance whatsoever, and the United States, Britain, and the Soviet Union all tried to blame one another for the dreadful destruction. Internal reports within the British and American governments were changed so many times, and so drastically, that the truth of how and why the bombing was sanctioned remains clouded to this day.*

Q. The heavily defended Japanese island of Iwo Jima, which had been bombed or bombarded from the sea intermittently since June of 1944, was given the full treatment from February 16 through the eighteenth in preparation for Marine landings on the nineteenth. What was the special strategic importance of Iwo Jima?

A. *Its three airfields were within range of Tokyo for fighter planes, which was not true of the American-held airfields in the Mariana Islands. If Iwo Jima could be taken, it would be possible for fighter planes stationed there to hook up with B-29s from the Marianas and serve as escorts on their bombing runs to Tokyo. In addition, it would be possible to use Iwo Jima as an emergency landing strip for bombers damaged on their missions to Tokyo.*

Q. How large was Iwo Jima?

    a. Eight square miles
    b. Fifteen square miles
    c. Twenty-five square miles

A. *It was only eight square miles, but the Japanese were so thoroughly dug in that it would have to be taken yard by yard.*

Q. What area of the island of Luzon in the Philippines was retaken on the twenty-first of February?

A. *Bataan.*

Q. Perhaps the most famous photograph of the entire war was that of U.S. Marines raising the American flag on Mount Suribachi on Iwo Jima on February 23, 1945. Was this the first or second flag raised on this site that day?

A. *It was the second. The first, only 54 by 24 inches, was raised at 10:30 A.M. under fairly heavy Japanese fire. As the day wore on, a much larger flag, 8 feet by 4 feet 4 inches, was brought from an offshore ship. This larger flag would be visible to U.S. troops much farther away. The raisings of both flags were photographed, but it was the second picture that became the model for the Marine Corps War Memorial in Arlington, Virginia. The taking of Mount Suribachi was only the beginning of the Iwo Jima campaign, however. It would be more than a month before the last Japanese were defeated.*

Q. In the Philippines, with casualties of nearly 1,000, the small island of Corregidor was taken on the twenty-sixth. It had been thought there were as few as 1,000 Japanese on the island, but there turned out to be 5,000. Since a small American force had managed to hold the island for four months in 1941, it was feared the battle would be long and hard. What did the Japanese do that brought about their own quick defeat?

A. *A Japanese plan to blast their way out was seriously bungled and tons of TNT blew up in their faces. A second explosion a few days later at an ammunition dump forced the Japanese out of their tunnels.*

Q. On March 2 a change of government took place in Romania. Who brought pressure for the change?

190

1945: Victory

A. *The Soviets insisted King Michael install a new Communist-dominated government. Stalin was already breaking the agreement he had made at Yalta to allow the Eastern European countries to form governments as they saw fit.*

Q. Why did the taking of the town of Meiktila in Burma by the British in early March make it inevitable that the Japanese would have to withdraw from Mandalay?

A. *Because the chief Japanese supply line was now cut.*

Q. Why did General MacArthur cancel his plans for a victory parade after the fall of Manila to the Allies on March 3?

A. *Because the city that had been called "the Pearl of the Orient" had been almost totally destroyed in the bitter fighting.*

Q. By March of 1945 the German manpower crisis was so severe that the army was forced to do what?

A. *Call upon fifteen- and sixteen-year-old boys to enter the ranks.*

Q. Second Lieutenant Karl Timmerman, of West Point, Nebraska, attached to the 9th Armored Division of the U.S. First Army in Europe, was the first man to cross what on March 7?

A. *He led his men across the Ludendorff Bridge over the Rhine River at Remagen, Germany. The Rhine, with its steep banks, was a natural defense line of the first magnitude. As the Allied armies approached the Rhine, the Germans re-*

191

treated across its bridges and then blew them up. But as the 9th Armored Division reached the hills above Remagen, troops were still crossing the bridge in retreat. The bridge itself was already wired with mines to blow it up, but Timmerman and his men crossed it anyway, on what could have been a suicide mission, while engineers cut the wires to the explosives. During the next ten days, five U.S. divisions crossed the bridge, which then collapsed, in part because of bomb damage but also from such heavy use.

Q. On the ninth, more than 300 B-29s flew in over Tokyo to deliver the greatest blow the Japanese homeland would receive in the course of the war, including the later drops of atomic bombs on Hiroshima and Nagasaki. At least 100,000 people were killed and more than a million were homeless, 60 percent of the business district was destroyed, and sixteen square miles of the city was gone. Why was the damage so great?

A. *More than 1,600 tons of incendiary bombs had been dropped by the B-29s onto the most densely populated area in the world, in Operation Meeting House, planned by General Curtis LeMay. The ground temperature rose so high that people burst into flame spontaneously. And because Japanese dwellings were largely constructed of wood and paper, the fire spread far beyond the targeted area. The justification for this attack was that vast numbers of homes were also small businesses that were producing materials essential to the Japanese war effort.*

Q. What March order of Hitler's did Albert Speer, the head of German industrial production, try to prevent from being put into effect?

A. *A scorched-earth policy, involving the destruction of everything in the advancing paths of the Allies when a position could no longer be held.*

Q. Had the Germans managed to build a bomber capable of flying all the way to the East Coast of the United States?

A. *Yes, but only two prototypes had been completed. Hitler had one at the ready to fly him to Japan if the military were to revolt against him again.*

Q. After a lull, kamikaze attacks by Japanese pilots were again on the rise. How many U.S. carriers were hit at the end of the third week of March?

A. *The* Franklin, *the* Wasp, *the* Enterprise, *and the* Essex *were all hit. The first two were put out of commission and the* Franklin *alone counted 832 dead, the worst toll since the sinking of the* Arizona *at Pearl Harbor.*

Q. As the fighting came to an end on Iwo Jima after only thirty-five days, it was all too clear that this campaign would deserve its Marine memorial. Why?

A. *There had been 18,000 American casualties, 6,000 of them fatal. The Japanese losses were staggering, with only 1 percent of a total garrison of over 20,000 still alive.*

Q. The last what landed in England on the twenty-seventh of March?

A. *V-2 rocket. While they were coming in, beginning on September 8, 1944, racing through the skies from Germany at 3,000 miles per hour, they were fearsome. About 1,250 of the rockets had been fired at England during that period, killing 9,000 and injuring 24,000. Another 30,000 casualties had occurred at Antwerp, which had been hit by 10,000 V-1s and 2,000 V-2s. But the toll could have been much*

193

higher. A raid by the RAF on the rocket research and manufacturing complex at Peenemünde on the Baltic in August of 1943 had set back the development of the rockets by several months. Now the Germans had been pushed too far back for the 200-mile range of the V-2s to be useful.

Q. What message sent to Stalin by General Eisenhower infuriated the British?

A. *In late March he advised Stalin that the American forces would be pushing forward through southern Germany instead of heading for Berlin. The British felt that this was politically unwise in that it would give the Soviets the upper hand in Berlin in terms of postwar settlements. Churchill protested to Roosevelt, but the decision was left to General Marshall, and he backed Eisenhower's plan. In hindsight, of course, the British were absolutely correct.*

Q. Also in late March, General Heinz Guderian was fired by Hitler as the Army Chief of Staff following a major fight about tactics. With what kind of officer did Hitler replace him?

A. *A man with less experience and talent, General Hans Krebs. It was something Hitler did again and again throughout the war.*

Q. What city, whose return to German rule Hitler had demanded in 1939, and into which he made a triumphal entry following the invasion of Poland, was captured by the Soviets on the thirtieth of March?

A. *Danzig, now known as Gdansk.*

1945: Victory

Q. The largest naval operation of the Pacific war began on April 1. What island was being invaded by the Allies?

A. *Okinawa. More than 450,000 army and Marine Corps troops were landed on the 700-square-mile island occupied by an equal number of Japanese civilians and 130,000 deeply entrenched soldiers. It was the Allies' intention to use Okinawa as a staging ground for the final attack on Japan.*

Q. On April 3, the last ships of Japan's once mighty fleet sailed toward Okinawa. The vast battleship *Yamato,* which had only barely survived the Battle of Leyte Gulf, led the way. What was the bizarre mission of the *Yamato?*

A. *It was to pound through the American fleet around Okinawa, causing as much damage as possible, and then beach itself on the island, with the 2,000 troops aboard to help reinforce the Japanese garrison. The Japanese ships were spotted by U.S. planes and a carrier-based air strike was mounted against them. Bombed and torpedoed nonstop for two hours, the largest battleship ever built sank in the South China Sea. Japan had ceased to be a naval power.*

Q. What event put Hitler in a rare joyous and optimistic mood on April 12?

A. *The news of the death at Warm Springs, Georgia, of President Franklin D. Roosevelt, of a cerebral hemorrhage. Hitler was at this point sufficiently deranged to say that the war could now be won.*

Q. "Any man in public life is bound, in the course of years, to create certain enmities. But when he is gone, his main objectives stand out clearly and one may hope that a spirit of

195

unity may arouse the people and their leaders to a complete understanding of his objectives and a determination to achieve those objectives themselves." Who wrote these words?

A. *Eleanor Roosevelt, in her daily newspaper column, after the death of her husband. When Harry Truman had arrived at the White House the evening of Roosevelt's death, he had asked Mrs. Roosevelt if there was anything he could do for her, and she had replied, "Is there anything we can do for you? For you are the one in trouble now."*

Q. Who quoted Longfellow's "Sail on, O ship of state" in a tribute to Roosevelt on the seventeenth of April?

A. *Winston Churchill, before a packed House of Commons.*

Q. Name the famous prisoner-of-war camp in Germany that was liberated by Allied forces on the seventeenth.

A. *Colditz.*

Q. In Italy the city of Bologna was finally taken from the Germans on the twenty-first of April. The Free troops of what country captured the city?

A. *Free Polish troops.*

Q. Heinrich Himmler passed a message to the Allies through the Red Cross on the twenty-second of April. What did it offer?

A. *It offered a surrender to the British and Americans, but excluded the Soviets. The Allies replied that they would ac-*

cept nothing but unconditional surrender. Hitler did not find out about this until the twenty-eighth. He called it "the most shameful betrayal in human history." He had already had Hermann Göring arrested for having the effrontery to state his willingness to take over if Hitler was unable to escape from Berlin.

Q. From what city in Burma did the Japanese begin to retreat on the last week of April?

A. *Rangoon. Indian and British divisions had been making rapid progress since retaking a large section of the Burma Road at the end of the previous month. The Burma war was nearly over.*

Q. Who, disguised as a German officer, was captured by Italian partisans as he tried to get from Italy into Switzerland on the twenty-seventh of April?

A. *Mussolini, who was captured together with his mistress, Clara Petacci. Both were shot the next day and their bodies were hung upside down in the Square of Martyrs in Milan. As they hung there a woman fired five more bullets into Mussolini's corpse, one for each of the five sons she had lost in the war.*

Q. What ceremony did Hitler have performed in his bunker in Berlin on the twenty-ninth of April as Soviet forces closed in on Berlin?

A. *He had a minor city official marry him to his mistress, Eva Braun. Joseph Goebbels, who had been at Hitler's side as Nazi propaganda minister from the start, and Martin Bor-*

197

mann, who had been Hitler's secretary since 1943, were witnesses.

Q. On the same day as Hitler's marriage, stunned and horrified soldiers from the U.S. Third Army liberated 30,000 people from what?

A. *Dachau. The first soldiers to arrive at the concentration camp were utterly unprepared for the walking skeletons they discovered within its confines. For many hardened soldiers who had fought their way across Europe through a rain of death, Dachau would be their worst memory of the entire war.*

Q. The following day, the thirtieth, Adolf Hitler had a light lunch of meatless spaghetti and salad with Eva Braun. In the midafternoon they committed suicide. What method did Hitler use?

A. *He bit into a capsule of cyanide and then shot himself in the head. Eva Braun took the cyanide alone. Their bodies were carried out of the bunker, doused with gasoline, and set aflame. The fact that they were cremated led the Allies to appoint a special commission after the war to make certain that Hitler was indeed dead. Their report, drawn from eyewitnesses and other evidence, showed conclusively that he was. But that has not prevented numerous novelists from resuscitating him since.*

Q. What did Magda, wife of Joseph Goebbels, do later in the afternoon?

A. *She fed her six children drugged candy and when they fell asleep, gave each of them a cyanide capsule, after which she and her husband followed suit.*

Q. What happened in Caserta, Italy, south of Rome, on the twenty-ninth?

A. *Overlooking one of the most beautiful formal gardens on earth, the Germans surrendered to the Allies. Negotiations for such a surrender had been in secret progress for many weeks, but the top commander in Italy, General Vietinghoff, did not agree to the terms until two days later, after the death of Hitler was formally announced in Berlin.*

Q. Who became the second Führer of the German Reich?

A. *Admiral Karl Doenitz, one of the few military leaders Hitler had not sacked at one time or another, was named successor in Hitler's will. His tenure would last only twenty-three days as he presided over the German surrender across the face of Europe.*

Q. The only bomb to hit the United States in the course of the war killed six people, all but one of them children, at the very late date of May 5. Where did this bomb come from?

A. *It was a Japanese "balloon bomb" sent aloft in the Pacific to be carried by the prevailing winds over the United States. Although many were put aloft, this one that fell on Oregon was the only one to find a target.*

Q. What was celebrated on May 8?

A. *VE Day, standing for Victory in Europe. The unconditional surrender had been signed the previous day at Eisenhower's headquarters in Reims, France.*

Q. The man whose name became a synonym for *traitor* was arrested by resistance fighters in what country on May 10?

A. *Vidkun Quisling was arrested in Norway, where he had served as Hitler's puppet. He would subsequently be convicted of treason and executed.*

Q. The battle for Okinawa continued unabated throughout the month of May, but progress was hindered by the usual very tough Japanese defense and by kamikaze attacks on the supporting naval fleet. How many kamikaze attacks were there in the month of May?

    a.   260
    b.   420
    c.   560

A. *The answer is c. In one such incident on May 11, two kamikaze planes hit the carrier* Bunker Hill *within thirty seconds of one another, setting the ship on fire. With extraordinary valor, the crew extinguished the blaze and saved the carrier. There were 392 dead and 264 wounded.*

Q. On the tenth of June, 30,000 troops from what country invaded Borneo?

A. *They were Australians. They were delighted to be given a mission of their own; General MacArthur had infuriated them by so often leaving them behind for tedious but extremely dangerous mop-up activities while he took American troops along to the next invasion. That was dangerous too, of course, but at least the American troops got some glory out of it.*

Q. Who was Lord Haw-Haw, and why was he put on trial in England in mid-June?

A. *Lord Haw-Haw was the derisive nickname for an English Nazi named William Joyce, who had broadcast propaganda from Germany throughout the war. He was convicted of treason and executed.*

Q. The battle for Okinawa came to a conclusion in the fourth week of June. There were nearly 50,000 American casualties, a quarter of them killed. How many times as many Japanese dead were there?

    a. Five times as many
    b. Ten times as many
    c. Thirteen times as many

A. *The answer is c; more than 40,000 of these were civilians. And although the U.S. forces had 763 planes shot down, the Japanese toll was as much as ten times that. U.S. naval damage was also very high, with several hundred ships damaged and 36 sunk. But the Japanese Navy no longer really existed.*

Q. What had representatives of several dozen countries spent the previous two months drafting in San Francisco?

A. *The Charter of the United Nations. Fifty countries signed it on the twenty-sixth of June.*

Q. What Broadway musical gave forty-three free performances for servicemen only between its opening in 1943 and the end of the war?

A. Oklahoma!

Q. Who wrote the "soldier's anthem" of World War II, "Praise the Lord and Pass the Ammunition"?

A. *Frank Loesser, who would go on to write* Guys and Dolls, The Most Happy Fella, *and* How to Succeed in Business Without Really Trying.

Q. What was the total number of American men and women who were in uniform at some point during the course of World War II?

A. *There were 16 million, almost two thirds of them in the army. There were over 4 million in the navy. The marines were the American equivalent of Britain's "The Few," the RAF pilots who fought the Battle of Britain. Although there were only a few more than 500,000 in the Marine Corps, they fought many of the war's most difficult battles on the islands of the Pacific.*

Q. In 1939, the federal budget had been a mere $9 billion. What was it in 1945?

A. *$100 billion.*

Q. At the end of June, with Okinawa firmly in U.S. hands and already being prepared as a launching base for attacks on the home islands of Japan, President Truman approved a date for the final assault. What was it?

A. *November 1.*

Q. Who was able to claim that his word had been kept on July 5, 1945?

A. *General MacArthur was able to announce that the Philippines had been totally liberated from the Japanese, thus fulfilling the promise he had made in February of 1942.*

Q. What could be seen and heard nearly two hundred miles away on the night of July 16?

A. *The test explosion of the first atomic bomb at Alamogordo in New Mexico.*

Q. Where did Harry Truman receive the news of the success of the atomic test?

A. *At Potsdam, a suburb of bombed-out Berlin, where he, Churchill, and Stalin began meetings on the seventeenth to discuss the shape of the postwar world. The telegram from Secretary of War Stimson read, "Diagnosis not yet complete but results seem satisfactory."*

Q. One of the following did *not* happen on July 26, 1945. Which is it?

   a. The results of the British election of July 5, which had been delayed in order to count the ballots of far-flung servicemen, were finally announced

   b. Truman decided to use the atomic bomb against Japan unless it surrendered soon

   c. A broadcast was made to the Japanese calling for unconditional surrender but making a strong point that the Allies did not intend to reduce Japan to a poverty-stricken nation

A. *The answer is b; Truman had made the decision to use the bomb two days earlier, which was why the new call for surrender was made to Japan. Truman had confided his decision to Churchill, and they had made a passing reference to Stalin concerning the existence of a new weapon without identifying what it was.*

   Churchill received the bitter news that the election, which the Labour party had insisted upon following the defeat of Germany, had cast him out of office. Around the world people were stunned at the lack of gratitude to the heroic wartime leader by the British people. But there was a reason. During the war, numerous new programs had been put in place in Britain to improve the life of the ordinary British citizen. For example, special nutritional programs for pregnant women had reduced the infant mortality rate in Britain despite severe rationing. There were dozens of such forward-looking efforts—the foundations of the welfare state—and most of them had been originated and administered by Labour party members of the coalition Cabinet. Amends would be made to Churchill in 1951 when he would again be elected prime minister.

Q. The cruiser *Indianapolis* was sunk by a Japanese submarine at the very end of July on a return voyage from the Mariana Islands. Why is it extremely fortunate—or unfortunate—that it was not sunk on its outward voyage?

A. *It carried the atomic bomb used on Hiroshima from the West Coast to the B-29 air base in the Marianas from which the attack would be launched.*

Q. On Pearl Harbor Day in 1941, a pilot in his mid-twenties heard the news as he was making a routine return to Langley Air Force Base in Virginia. Where was he on August 6, 1945, and what was his name?

A. *On August 6, 1945, Colonel Paul W. Tibbets, Jr., was piloting a revamped B-29 (which he had named* Enola Gay *after his mother) on a mission to drop the first atomic bomb on Hiroshima. He had distinguished himself as a bomber pilot in Europe, but this was something very different, for he had been told exactly what he was carrying. "Fat Man" it was called, a uranium fission bomb fourteen feet long and five feet in diameter. It would kill 80,000 people, many of them instantly, and many more in years to come because of the effects of the radiation it produced.*

Q. A second atomic bomb, of the more advanced plutonium type, was dropped on Nagasaki on the ninth, after new warnings of further devastation if the Japanese did not surrender. The city of Nagasaki was the secondary target—after Kokura, where cloud cover prevented a strike—and even there the cloud cover was so great that the bomb fell three miles off target. The devastation was still enormous, but there was something else that happened that day that was at least equally important in bringing about the Japanese surrender. What was it?

A. *Stalin finally kept his promise and, after declaring war the day before, launched a million and a half troops against the Japanese defenses in Manchuria. The Japanese Army had tried to keep the bombing of Hiroshima secret and then to dismiss the idea that it was an atomic bomb rather than an augmented conventional weapon. But with the bombing of Nagasaki and the devastating Soviet attack, the picture changed. The Japanese stalled for four days, and then Emperor Hirohito himself demanded an end to the war. He personally recorded the message of surrender, and it was broadcast on August 14—VJ Day to the Allies.*

Q. At the signing of the Japanese surrender in Tokyo harbor on September 2, 1945, presided over by General MacArthur, there were two generals who did not look like military leaders. One was British and one was American. Who were they?

A. *Rail-thin and just released by the Japanese, General Jonathan Wainwright, who had surrendered at Corregidor, and General A. E. Perceval, who had surrendered at Singapore, were accorded the honor of being present at the surrender. Despite their long imprisonment, they could count themselves extremely fortunate.*

Q. Poland had been invaded by the Nazis five years and one day before the Japanese surrender was signed in Tokyo Harbor. Averaged out over the 260 weeks the war lasted, how many people were killed for each week of World War II?

A. *Based on what some consider a low estimate of 50 million dead, the toll was an average of 192,307 for each week of the war. The slaughter of the Jews in death camps was the most repugnant and horrifying, but the Russian losses were three times as great . . . and further statistical breakdown seems beside the point—192,307 for every week of the war. "Praise the Lord and Pass the Ammunition."*

Bibliography

Bailey, Ronald H. *The Home Front: U.S.A*. New York: Time-Life Books, Inc., 1978.

Baldwin, Hanson. *Battles Lost and Won*. New York: Harper & Row, 1966.

―――. *The Crucial Years: 1939–41*. New York: Harper & Row, 1976.

Baudot, Marcel, et al., eds. *The Historical Encyclopedia of World War II*. New York: Facts on File, Inc., 1989.

Brinkley, David. *Washington Goes to War*. New York: Knopf, 1988.

Bryant, Arthur. *The Triumph in the West*. Garden City, N.Y.: Doubleday & Company, 1959.

―――. *The Turn of the Tide*. Garden City, N.Y.: Doubleday & Company, 1957.

Burns, James MacGregor. *Roosevelt: The Soldier of Freedom*. New York: Harcourt Brace Jovanovich, 1970.

Churchill, Winston S. *Blood, Sweat and Tears*. New York: Putnam's, 1941.

―――. *The Second World War, Vol. III: The Grand Alliance*. Boston: Houghton Mifflin, 1950.

Colville, John. *The Fringes of Power: 10 Downing Street Diaries 1939–1955*. New York: Norton, 1985.

Costello, John. *The Pacific War, 1941–45*. New York: Quill, 1982.

de Bedts, Ralph F. *Recent American History: 1933 Through World War II*. Homewood, Ill.: The Dorsey Press, 1973.

Dupuy, Trevor Nevitt. *Combat Leaders of World War II*. New York: Franklin Watts, 1965.

Editors of Time-Life Books. *WWII*. New York: Time-Life Books, 1989.

Eisenhower, Dwight D. *Crusade in Europe*. Garden City, N.Y.: Doubleday & Company, 1948.

Englemann, Bernt. *In Hitler's Germany: Daily Life in the Third Reich*. New York: Pantheon, 1986.

Esposito, Vincent J., ed. *A Concise History of World War II*. New York: Praeger, 1964.

Fermi, Laura. *Atoms in the Family*. Chicago: Chicago University Press, 1950.

Fuller, John F. C. *The Second World War, 1939–1945: A Strategical and Tactical History*. New York: Duell, Sloan and Pearce, 1949.

Gallo, Max. *Mussolini's Italy: Twenty Years of the Facist Era*. New York: Macmillan, 1964.

Groves, Leslie. *Now It Can Be Told*. New York: Harper & Row, 1962.

Gurney, Gene. *The War in the Air*. New York: Bonanza Books, 1962.

Heckman, Wold. *Rommel's War in Africa*. Garden City, N.Y.: Doubleday & Company, 1981.

Heiferman, Ronald. *World War II*. London: Octopus Books, Ltd., 1972.

Hoyt, Edwin P. *How They Won the War in the Pacific*. New York: Weybright and Talley, 1971.

Ickes, Harold. *The Secret Diary of Harold L. Ickes, Vol. II*. New York: Simon & Schuster, 1954.

Jablonski, Edward. *Airwar*. Garden City, N.Y.: Doubleday & Company, 1959.

Bibliography

James, D. Clayton. *The Years of MacArthur, Vol. II, 1941–1945*. Boston: Houghton Mifflin, 1975.

Jones, R. V. *The Wizard War: British Scientific Intelligence, 1939–1945*. New York: Coward, McCann, 1978.

Keegan, John. *The Second World War*. New York: Viking, 1989.

Lewin, Ronald. *The American Magic: Codes, Ciphers and the Defeat of Japan*. New York: Farrar, Straus & Giroux, 1982.

Liddell Hart, B. H. *The History of the Second World War*. New York: Putnam's, 1971.

Macksey, Kenneth. *The Partisans of Europe in the Second World War*. New York: Stein & Day, 1975.

Malone, Dumas, and Basil Rauch. *America and World Leadership, 1940–1965*. New York: Meredith Publishing Company, 1965.

Manchester, William. *The Glory and the Dream*. Boston: Little, Brown, 1974.

Merill, James M. *A Sailor's Admiral: A Biography of William F. Halsey*. New York: Thomas Y. Crowell, 1976.

Montgomery, Bernard Law. *The Memoirs of Field Marshal the Viscount Montgomery of Alamein*. Cleveland: World Publishing, 1958.

Moser, Don. *China-Burma-India*. New York: Time-Life Books, 1978.

Payne, Robert. *The Life and Death of Adolf Hitler*. New York: Praeger, 1973.

Persico, Joseph E. *Piercing the Reich*. New York: Ballantine Books, 1979.

Pogue, Forrest C. *Organizer of Victory, 1943–1945: George C. Marshall*. New York: Viking, 1973.

Prange, Gordon W. *At Dawn We Slept*. New York: Penguin, 1982.

Reader's Digest Illustrated Story of World War II. Pleasantville, N.Y.: The Reader's Digest Association, 1969.

Roosevelt, Eleanor. *My Day*. New York: Phoros Books, 1989.

Rumph, Hans. *The Bombing of Germany*. New York: Holt, Rinehart & Winston, 1961.

Ryan, Cornelius. *The Last Battle*. New York: Simon & Schuster, 1966.

Seaton, Albert. *The Battle for Moscow, 1941–1942*. New York: Stein and Day, 1971.

Shirer, William. *The Rise and Fall of the Third Reich*. New York: Simon & Schuster, 1960.

Sinkins, Peter. *Illustrated Book of World War II*. New York: St. Martin's Press, 1972.

Sommerville, Donald. *World War II Day by Day*. Greenwich, Conn.: Dorset Press, 1989.

Spector, Ronald H. *Eagle Against the Sun*. New York: The Free Press, 1985.

Steel, Ronald. *Walter Lippmann and the American Century*. Boston: Atlantic-Little, Brown, 1980.

Steinberg, Rafael. *Return to the Philippines*. New York: Time-Life Books, 1979.

Stroop, Juergen, translated and annotated by Sybil Milton. *The Stroop Report*. New York: Pantheon Books, 1979.

Taylor, A.J.P., ed. *History of World War II*. London: Octopus Books, 1974.

Thompson, Lawrence. *1940*. New York: William Morrow & Company, 1966.

Toland, John. *The Rising Sun*. New York: Bantam Books, 1971.

Trevor-Roper, H. R. *Blitzkrieg to Defeat*. New York: Holt, Rinehart & Winston, 1965.

Truman, Margaret. *Harry S. Truman*. New York: William Morrow & Company, 1973.

Tunner, William H. *Over the Hump*. New York: Duell, Sloan and Pearce, 1964.

U.S. Department of the Army. *American Military History 1607–1953, ROTCM 145–20*. Washington: Department of the Army, 1956.

Warner, Philip. *World War II: The Untold Story*. London: The Bodley Head, 1988.

Zhukov, Georgei. *The Memoirs of Marshal Zhukov*. New York: Delacorte, 1971.